In-Depth Resources: Unit 5

World War II and Its Aftermath

McDougal Littell
A HOUGHTON MIFFLIN COMPANY
Evanston, Illinois • Boston • Dallas

Acknowledgments

CHAPTER 16

Excerpt from *Sophie's Choice* by William Styron. Copyright © 1979 by William Styron. Reprinted by permission of Random House, Inc.

CHAPTER 17

Excerpt from *Farewell to Manzanar* by James D. Houston and Jeanne Wakatsuki Houston. Copyright © 1973 by James D. Houston. Reprinted by permission of Houghton Mifflin Company. All rights reserved.

Excerpt from *Ernie's War: The Best of Ernie Pyle's World War II Dispatches,* edited by David Nichols. Reprinted by permission of the Scripps-Howard Foundation.

Excerpt from "Atom Bomb Loosed on Nagasaki" by William L. Laurence in *The New York Times,* August 9, 1945. Copyright 1945 by The New York Times Company. Reprinted by permission of The New York Times.

Excerpt from *Snow Falling on Cedars* by David Guterson. Copyright © 1994 by David Guterson. Reprinted by permission of Harcourt Brace & Company.

CHAPTER 18

Excerpt from *Letters from Father: The Truman Family's Personal Correspondence* by Margaret Truman. Copyright © 1981 by Margaret Truman. By permission of William Morrow and Company, Inc.

Excerpt from *The Nuclear Age* by Tim O'Brien. Copyright © 1985 by Tim O'Brien. Reprinted by permission of Alfred A. Knopf, Inc.

CHAPTER 19

Excerpt from *The Other America* by Michael Harrington. Copyright © 1962, 1969, 1981 by Michael Harrington. Reprinted with the permission of Simon & Schuster.

"Relocation," from *Cherokee Stories* by the Reverend Watt Spade and Willard Walker with Alec England, Lizzy England, Juanita Crittenden, Johnson Tehee, and Sam H. Hair. Illustrated by Jim Redcorn. Published by Wesleyan University Laboratory of Anthropology. Copyright © 1966 by the Carnegie Corporation Cross-Cultural Education Project of the University of Chicago. Reprinted by permission of Willard Walker.

Excerpt from *1959* by Thulani Davis. Copyright © 1992 by Thulani Davis. Reprinted by permission of Grove/Atlantic, Inc.

Printed in the United States of America.

ISBN-13: 978-0-618-17610-6   ISBN-10: 0-618-17610-1

8 9 10 11 12 – MDO – 08 07 06

CHAPTER 18 Cold War Conflicts, 1945–1960

CHAPTER 19 The Postwar Boom, 1946–1960

CHAPTER

16

Section 1

GUIDED READING *Dictators Threaten World Peace*

A. As you read this section, take notes about the rise of dictators in Europe and Asia.

	1. Joseph Stalin	**2. Benito Mussolini**	**3. Adolf Hitler**
Nation			
Political movement and beliefs			
Aggressive actions taken in the 1920s and 1930s			

	4. Japanese Militarists	**5. Francisco Franco**
Nation		
Political movement and beliefs		
Aggressive actions taken in the 1920s and 1930s		

B. On the back of this paper, define **totalitarian.** Then explain the significance of the **Neutrality Acts.**

Name _____ Date _____

A. As you read this section, take notes to answer questions about how Germany
started World War II. Note the development of events in the time line.

1938		
March	**Germany invades Austria.**	1. Why did Neville Chamberlain sign the Munich Pact?
September	**Munich Pact is signed by Germany, France, and Britain.** →	2. Why did Winston Churchill oppose the pact?

1939

March — **Germany invades Czechoslovakia.**

3. What did Germany and the USSR agree to in their accords?

August — **Germany and USSR sign nonaggression pact and secret agreement.** →

September — **Germany invades Poland.** →

4. What happened to Poland as a result of the invasion, and how did Britain and France respond to it?

November — **USSR invades Finland.**

1940

Spring — **Germany invades Norway, Denmark, the Netherlands, Belgium, and Luxembourg.**

5. What were the surrender terms offered to France?

June — **France surrenders to Germany.** →

Summer — **USSR overruns Baltic states.**

6. What type of battle was the Battle of Britain, and why was England's victory so important?

Battle of Britain begins. →

B. On the back of this paper, identify who **Charles de Gaulle** was. Then define
appeasement, nonaggression pact, and **blitzkrieg.**

CHAPTER 16

Section 3

GUIDED READING *The Holocaust*

A. As you read, take notes to answer questions related to the time line.

1925	In *Mein Kampf,* Hitler presents his racist views on "Aryans" and Jews.	
1933	Hitler comes to power. Soon after, he orders non-Aryans to be removed from government jobs and begins to build concentration camps.	
	Thousands of Jews begin leaving Germany. →	1. Why didn't France and Britain accept as many German Jews as they might have?
1935	Nuremberg laws are → passed.	2. What did the Nuremberg laws do?
1938	*Kristallnacht* occurs. →	3. What happened during *Kristallnacht?*
1939	As war breaks out in Europe, U.S. Coast → Guard prevents refugees on the *St. Louis* from landing in Miami.	4. Why didn't the United States accept as many German Jews as it might have?
1941	Nazis build six death → camps in Poland.	5. What groups did the Nazis single out for extermination?
1945 to 1949	After war in Europe ends in 1945, many → Nazi leaders are brought to justice for their crimes against humanity.	6. How did the Nazis go about exterminating the approximately 11 million people who died in the Holocaust?

B. On the back of this paper, define **genocide**.

CHAPTER 16

Section 4

GUIDED READING *America Moves Toward War*

As you read, take notes about how the United States entered World War II.

1939	Congress passes Neutrality Act. →	1. What did the Neutrality Act allow?
1940	Axis powers form alliance. →	2. Who were the Axis powers? What did their alliance mean for the United States?
1941	Congress passes Lend-Lease Act. Germany invades USSR. →	3. What did the Lend-Lease Act do?
	Japan takes over French military bases in Indochina. → Congress extends the draft.	4. What did the United States do to protest Japan's action?
	Churchill and Roosevelt draft the Atlantic Charter. →	5. What pledges were contained in the Atlantic Charter?
	"A Declaration by the United Nations" is signed by the Allies. → Hideki Tojo becomes Japan's prime minister.	6. Who were the Allies?
	U.S. Senate allows arming of merchant ships. Japan launches a surprise attack on Pearl Harbor. →	7. What did the attack do to the U.S. Pacific fleet?
	As U.S. declares war on Japan, Germany and Italy declare war on U.S. →	8. Why did Germany and Italy declare war on the United States?

CHAPTER 16 · BUILDING VOCABULARY *World War Looms*

A. Matching Match the description in the second column with person in the first column. Write the appropriate letter next to the word.

_____ 1. Neville Chamberlain   a. British prime minister during World War II

_____ 2. Hideki Tojo   b. totalitarian ruler of Soviet Union

_____ 3. Benito Mussolini   c. ruler of French government in exile

_____ 4. Francisco Franco   d. leader of Nazi Party

_____ 5. Winston Churchill   e. led fascist rebellion in Spain

_____ 6. Joseph Stalin   f. agreed to Hitler's Sudetenland invasion

_____ 7. Charles de Gaulle   g. called himself *Il Duce*

_____ 8. Adolf Hitler   h. Japanese prime minister

B. Completion Select the term or name that best completes the sentence.

fascism	u-boat	*blitzkrieg*
Atlantic Charter	appeasement	totalitarian
Axis Powers	Lend-Lease Act	Allies

1. A _____ government is one that maintains complete control over its citizens.

2. _____ is a form a government that stresses nationalism and places the interests of the state above those of the individual.

3. Germany's military strategy, known as _____, relied on quick strikes with the use of advanced weaponry.

4. Germany, Italy, and Japan comprised a coalition known as the _____.

5. The measure that enabled the United States to provide arms and other supplies to Great Britain and its allies was known as the _____.

C. Writing Write a paragraph about the Holocaust using the following names and terms.

genocide   **ghetto**   **concentration camp**

CHAPTER 16

Section 2

SKILLBUILDER PRACTICE *Developing Historical Perspective*

How did Adolf Hitler, seen as a madman by many today, manage to come to power in Germany? Read this excerpt from a speech Hitler gave to German munitions workers near the end of 1940, and try to hear his words as the audience did—that is, without the knowledge history gives. Then answer the questions at the bottom of the page. (See Skillbuilder Handbook, p. R11.)

We find ourselves amid a controversy which aims at more than victory of one or another country. In fact, it is a struggle of two worlds. Forty-six million English rule and govern a total territory of roughly 40,000,000 square kilometres in this world. Eighty-five million Germans have a living space of hardly 600,000 square kilometres and these only through our own initiative. This earth, however, was not distributed by Providence or by almighty God.

This distribution is being taken care of by the peoples themselves, and this distribution chiefly took place in the past 300 years at a time when our German people were domestically unconscious and torn apart.

The right to live constitutes a claim of fundamental nature. The right to live includes the right to the soil, which alone gives life. For this claim, peoples have even fought when a lack of wisdom threatened to interfere with their relationship for they knew that even bloody sacrifices are better than the gradual dying of the nations. National unity was our first demand. Piece by piece and move by move this was realized. . . .

Our ideal is that every position in the country shall be filled by a true son of the people. We want a State in which birth matters nothing, achievement means everything. For this we are working with tremendous fanaticism. Contrasted with this is the idea of our enemies—a fight for egoism, for capital, for individual and family privileges. . . .

How often have I stretched out my hand! I was not in any mood to arm. That devours so much labor power. I wanted to use German labor power for other plans. My ambition is to make the German people rich and the German land beautiful. I would like us to have the most beautiful and the best culture. I was determined to rear our structure in the world, to widen our position and, secondly, to arm at home so that the German soldier must no longer stand alone on the front, lonely and the victim of superior forces.

Then I did everything humanly possible to avoid conflict. I made offer after offer to the English, but there wasn't anything to be done— they wanted war. For seven years Churchill said "I want war." Now he has it.

from Adolf Hitler's speech, reprinted in *Time* (December 23, 1940), 17–18.

1. Hitler referred to a number of subjects that appealed to the emotions of his audience. List some of those appeals.

   _____

   _____

   _____

2. What do the topics Hitler chose to speak on tell you about the needs and views of the people in his audience?

   _____

   _____

   _____

CHAPTER
16
Section 1

RETEACHING ACTIVITY *Dictators Threaten World Peace*

Reading Comprehension

Choose the best answer for each item. Write the letter of your answer in the blank.

_____ 1. Nationalism is an intense loyalty to one's
   a. family.
   b. race.
   c. religion.
   d. country.

_____ 2. Throughout the 1930s, dictators seized control in many countries, but not in
   a. Germany.
   b. France.
   c. Italy.
   d. Japan.

_____ 3. Benito Mussolini began building his new "Roman Empire" by seizing
   a. Ethiopia.
   b. Manchuria.
   c. Spain.
   d. the Rhineland.

_____ 4. On the eve of World War II, Italy and Germany helped fascist forces win a civil war in
   a. Spain.
   b. China.
   c. Japan.
   d. Ethiopia.

_____ 5. President Franklin Roosevelt's Good Neighbor policy applied to
   a. Asia.
   b. Canada.
   c. Great Britain.
   d. Latin America.

_____ 6. America's Neutrality Acts outlawed arms sales to
   a. fascist countries.
   b. Communist countries.
   c. all European countries.
   d. all countries at war.

CHAPTER 16

Section 2

RETEACHING ACTIVITY *War in Europe*

A. Sequencing Put the events below in the correct chronological order.

_____ 1. Britain and France declare war on Germany.

_____ 2. Battle of Britain.

_____ 3. Britain, France, and Germany sign the Munich Agreement.

_____ 4. Hitler invades Denmark and Norway.

_____ 5. Germany invades Poland.

_____ 6. France surrenders to Germany.

B. Completion Select the term or name that best completes the sentence.

Austria	natural resources	*blitzkrieg*
air force	navy	nonaggression pact
Axis Powers	phony war	Poland

1. On the eve of the outbreak of war, Germany and the Soviet Union signed a _____, in which they vowed never to attack each other.

2. The first country conquered in Hitler's "lightning war" was _____.

3. The months-long lull in the war almost right after it began was referred to by newspapers as the _____.

4. Hitler sought to annex Czechoslovakia to provide more living space for Germans and control the region's important _____.

5. Britain repelled Germany's attack due mainly to the heroic effort by its _____.

CHAPTER 16

Section 3

RETEACHING ACTIVITY *The Holocaust*

Finding Main Ideas

The following questions deal with the Holocaust. Answer them in the space provided.

1. Why were the Jews especially targeted by the Nazis?

_____

_____

2. What was the *Kristallnacht*?

_____

_____

3. Why was the United States willing to accept only a limited number of Jewish refugees?

_____

_____

4. How did Jews in the ghettos challenge the Nazis?

_____

_____

5. What was the "Final Solution" and why was it implemented?

_____

_____

6. What methods did the Nazi use to kill the occupants of their concentration camps?

_____

_____

Name _____ Date _____

Summarizing

A. Complete the chart below by summarizing the significance of each entry.

Event	Significance
Lend-Lease Act	
Atlantic Charter	
Attack on Pearl Harbor	

Main Ideas

B. Answer the following questions in the space provided.

1. How did the United States react to the early Nazi victories in Europe?

_____

_____

2. How did the United States respond to Japanese aggression in Asia?

_____

_____

3. Why did Japan launch an attack on U.S. naval forces at Pearl Harbor?

_____

_____

CHAPTER 16

Section 4

GEOGRAPHY APPLICATION: REGION *Japanese Aggression*

Directions: Read the paragraph below and study the map carefully. Then answer the questions that follow.

Japan, a densely populated country with few natural resources, substantially increased its territory in the late 1800s and early 1900s. Primarily as a result of wars with Russia and China, Japan gained "living space" during these years: the Kuril Islands (1875), the island of Taiwan (1895), Korea (1905), and the southern half of Sakhalin Island (1905). By 1931, Japanese militarists had thwarted the civilian government and begun seizing still more land. This time the emphasis was on controlling areas that held resources vital to the Japanese economy. Over the next ten years, targets included the Chinese region of Manchuria, rich in coal and iron, and the Dutch East Indies, with its abundant oil fields.

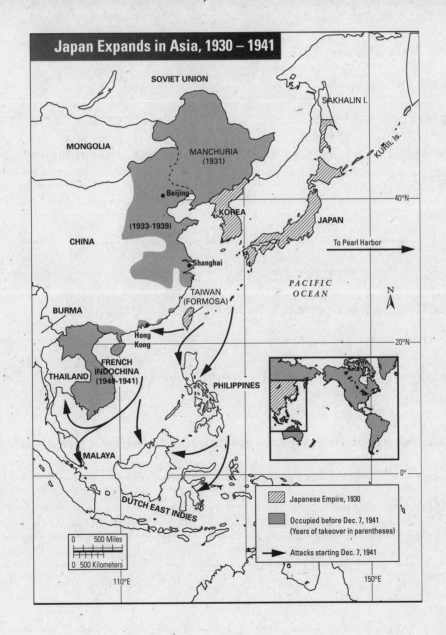

Japan Expands in Asia, 1930 – 1941

SOVIET UNION

SAKHALIN I.

MONGOLIA

MANCHURIA (1931)

KURIL Is.

Beijing

40°N

KOREA

JAPAN

(1933-1939)

To Pearl Harbor

CHINA

Shanghai

PACIFIC OCEAN

TAIWAN (FORMOSA)

N

BURMA

Hong Kong

20°N

FRENCH INDOCHINA (1940-1941)

THAILAND

PHILIPPINES

MALAYA

0°

DUTCH EAST INDIES

Japanese Empire, 1930

Occupied before Dec. 7, 1941 (Years of takeover in parentheses)

Attacks starting Dec. 7, 1941

0   500 Miles

0   500 Kilometers

110°E

150°E

Interpreting Text and Visuals

1. Describe Japan's empire as it existed in 1930. _____

_____

2. Where did Japan first expand its empire after 1930? _____

_____

Why do you think Japan targeted this region? _____

_____

_____

3. Describe the extent of Japanese influence in China in 1938. _____

_____

_____

4. What advantage did its control of French Indochina give Japan in attacks starting
on December 7, 1941? _____

_____

_____

_____

5. Japan seized Hong Kong on December 8, 1941. From where was the attack
mounted? _____

6. Which objective of the attacks starting on December 7, 1941 is outside the area
shown in the map? _____

7. What do you think made the Philippines a particularly attractive target for Japanese expansion?

_____

_____

_____

_____

PRIMARY SOURCE *from* Franklin D. Roosevelt's "Quarantine Speech"

During a tour of the nation in 1937 to drum up support for his domestic programs, President Roosevelt delivered a speech in which he indicated a shift in foreign policy. As you read this excerpt from his speech, consider why he felt the United States could no longer cling to isolationism and nonintervention.

It is because the people of the United States under modern conditions must, for the sake of their own future, give thought to the rest of the world, that I, as the responsible executive head of the nation, have chosen this great inland city [Chicago] and this gala occasion to speak to you on a subject of definite national importance. . . .

There is a solidarity and interdependence about the modern world, both technically and morally, which makes it impossible for any nation completely to isolate itself from economic and political upheavals in the rest of the world, especially when such upheavals appear to be spreading and not declining. There can be no stability or peace either within nations or between nations except under laws and moral standards adhered to by all. International anarchy destroys every foundation for peace. It jeopardizes either the immediate or the future security of every nation, large or small. It is, therefore, a matter of vital interest and concern to the people of the United States that the sanctity of international treaties and the maintenance of international morality be restored.

The overwhelming majority of the peoples and nations of the world today want to live in peace. . . .

I am compelled and you are compelled, nevertheless, to look ahead. The peace, the freedom, and the security of 90 percent of the population of the world is being jeopardized by the remaining 10 percent who are threatening a breakdown of all international order and law. Surely the 90 percent who want to live in peace under law and in accordance with moral standards that have received almost universal acceptance through the centuries can and must find some way to make their will prevail. . . .

It seems to be unfortunately true that the epidemic of world lawlessness is spreading. When an epidemic of physical disease starts to spread, the community approves and joins in a quarantine of the patients in order to protect the health of the community against the spread of the disease.

It is my determination to pursue a policy of peace and to adopt every practicable measure to avoid involvement in war. It ought to be inconceivable that in this modern era, and in the face of experience, any nation could be so foolish and ruthless as to run the risk of plunging the whole world into war by invading and violating, in convention of solemn treaties, the territory of other nations that have done them no real harm and which are too weak to protect themselves adequately. Yet the peace of the world and the welfare and security of every nation is today being threatened by that very thing.

War is a contagion, whether it be declared or undeclared. It can engulf states and peoples remote from the original scene of hostilities. We are determined to keep out of war, yet we cannot insure ourselves against the disastrous effects of war and the dangers of involvement. We are adopting such measures as will minimize our risk of involvement, but we cannot have complete protection in a world of disorder in which confidence and security have broken down.

If civilization is to survive, the principles of the Prince of Peace must be restored. Shattered trust between nations must be revived. Most important of all, the will for peace on the part of peace-loving nations must express itself to the end that nations that may be tempted to violate their agreements and the rights of others will desist from such a cause. There must be positive endeavors to preserve peace.

from Franklin D. Roosevelt, *Congressional Record Appendix,* 75th Congress, 2nd Session, 20–21.

Discussion Questions

1. Why did Roosevelt believe the U.S. could not isolate itself from the rest of the world?
2. What was the epidemic of "world lawlessness" that Roosevelt referred to in this speech?
3. Do you agree with the sentiments expressed in this speech? Explain your opinion.

PRIMARY SOURCE The Bombing of Pearl Harbor

On December 7, 1941, First Sergeant Roger Emmons witnessed the Japanese attack on Pearl Harbor. As you read this excerpt from his eyewitness account, think about the effects of the surprise assault.

It was a beautiful morning with fleecy clouds in the sky, and the visibility was good. Aboard the *Tennessee* the usual Sunday schedule prevailed. Many of the officers had gone ashore over the weekend. The Marine Detachment was drawn up on the fantail for morning Colors, mess tables were being cleared away, some of the men were getting dressed preparatory to going on liberty, while others "batted-the-breeze" over their after-breakfast smoke. In its beginning the day was just another peaceful Sunday at the United States' largest naval base.

A few minutes before 7:55 A.M., several squadrons of mustard-yellow planes flew over the Hawaiian island of Oahu from the southwest, but this caused no alarm as military planes overhead were the usual thing. When those squadrons approached Pearl Harbor, they maneuvered into attack formations at low altitude over Merry's Point. At 7:55 A.M. wave after wave of those warplanes streamed across the harbor and hurled their deadly missiles upon the unsuspecting battle fleet. Every plane seemed to have its objective selected in advance, for they separated into groups and each group concentrated on a specific ship.

When the first wave of attacking planes came over, I was in the Marine Detachment office on the second deck of the *Tennessee.* Pfc. George W. Dinning, the clerk, was seated at the desk making out the Morning Report. Suddenly we felt a violent bump which gave us the feeling that the ship had been pushed bodily sideways, and as I did not hear any explosion I remarked that some ship had run into us.

Immediately after that the alarm gongs sounded "General Quarters." I was so surprised that I could hardly believe my ears, but the noise of explosions through the open ports forced it upon me. George never did finish that Morning Report; he jumped seemingly sideways through the door and was gone like the wind. Snatching a detachment roster from the desk, I dashed after him.

My battle station was on the 5-inch broadside guns where I could see what actually was happening around us. I had a hurried look round from the casemates on the starboard side and then went over

to the port side. The sky was dotted with black puffs of antiaircraft fire. A plane, trailing a plume of smoke, was plunging earthward over Ford Island. Off in the direction of Schofield Barracks, there was a vast cloud of black smoke. At the same time, two billowing pillars of smoke arose from the Navy Yard and Hickam Field area. The sky was full of planes bearing the Rising Sun emblem of Japan. Overhead droned a flight of horizontal bombers at an altitude of about 10,000 feet. Some sixty enemy planes were diving at our ships.

Then a great many things happened in a very short time. The Japanese planes struck time and time again to get in the killing blows. First came aerial torpedoes, then heavy bombers and dive bombers. Within a few minutes of the commencement of the attack, we were hit direct two times by bombs.

One bomb bursting on the forward turret disabled one gun, and a fragment from it penetrated the shield on the bridge above, killing a sailor and severely wounding Ensign Donald M. Kable. The commander of the *West Virginia*, Captain Mervyn S. Bennion, was mortally wounded by a portion of this bomb when he emerged from the conning tower to the bridge of his ship. The second (a 15- or 16-inch projectile, which the enemy was using as a bomb) hit the aft turret, but fortunately, it did not explode, but pierced the top, killing two men under the point of impact.

At about 8:00 A.M., a terrific explosion in the *Arizona*, astern of us, fairly lifted us in the water. She blew up in an enormous flame and a cloud of black smoke when her forward magazine exploded after a Japanese bomb had literally dropped down her funnel. Her back broken by the explosion, the entire forward portion of the ship canted away from the aft portion as the ship began to settle on the bottom.

It was a scene which cannot easily be forgotten— the *Arizona* was a mass of fire from bow to foremast, on deck and between decks, and the surface of the water for a large distance round was a mass of flaming oil from millions of gallons of fuel oil. Over a thousand dead men lay in her twisted wreck. Among those who perished were Rear Admiral Isaac C.

Kidd and Captain Franklin Van Valkenburgh.

A few moments after this disaster, our attention was absorbed in the *Oklahoma*. Stabbed several times in her port side by torpedoes, she heeled very gently over, and capsized within nine minutes. The water was dotted with the heads of men. Some swam ashore, covered from head to foot with thick, oily scum, but hundreds of men trapped in the vessel's hull were drowned.

We had only been in the attack a few minutes when the *West Virginia,* about 20 feet on our port beam, began slowly to settle by the bow, and then took a heavy list to the port. She had been badly hit by several torpedoes in the opening attack. Incendiary bombs started fires which filled her decks and superstructure with flame and smoke.

In the midst of all this turmoil, the *Nevada,* the next ship astern of the blazing *Arizona,* got under way and headed for the channel. As she moved down stream, the vessel was a target of many enemy planes until badly crippled by a torpedo, and after that she ran aground to prevent sinking.

The next picture was a destroyer, name unknown, leaving the harbor under a withering fire from Japanese planes.

But to return to the *Tennessee*. The real story of this ship lies in the splendid manner in which the officers and men on board arose to the emergency. When "General Quarters" was sounded, all hands dashed to their battle stations. There was no panic. The shock found each and every man ready for his job. Antiaircraft and machine guns were quickly manned, the first gun getting into action in less than three minutes after the alarm.

For the next forty minutes, the *Tennessee* was the center of a whirlwind of bombs and bullets. The Japanese planes bombed our ship and then bombed again. They opened up with machine guns in low flying attacks. The ship's gun crews fought with utmost gallantry, and in a most tenacious and

determined manner. . . . Hostile planes swooping down on what they thought an easy prey were greeted with volleys from our antiaircraft and machine guns. After such a warm reception, the Japanese gave the *Tennessee* a wide berth.

So terrific was the noise of explosions and our own antiaircraft guns that one could not hear himself speak and had to shout in anybody's ear. The air seemed to be full of fragments and flying pieces. In the general din, there was a *whoosh,* followed by a dull *whoomph* of huge explosives which struck so close to the ship that she shivered from end to end.

from Roger Emmons, "Pearl Harbor," *Marine Corps Gazette,* XXVIII (February 1944). Reprinted in Richard B. Morris and James Woodress, eds., *Voices from America's Past,* vol. 3, The Twentieth Century (New York: Dutton, 1962), 148–151.

Research Options

1. Find out more about the attack on Pearl Harbor. How did the Japanese avoid detection? Why was the United States unprepared for a sneak attack? When did the Japanese formally declare war on the United States? How did Congress respond to Roosevelt's request to declare war on Japan? Prepare a brief oral report and share it with your classmates.

2. Find and read President Roosevelt's address to Congress on December 8, 1941 or the text of his December 9 radio broadcast to the American people. Then discuss with classmates whether his remarks were consistent with what he said in his "quarantine speech" in 1937.

3. With a small group of classmates, brainstorm an appropriate memorial for the men who were killed during the attack on Pearl Harbor. Then find out about the U.S.S. *Arizona* National Memorial to compare your ideas with this memorial at Pearl Harbor, Oahu.

CHAPTER **16**

Section 4

PRIMARY SOURCE War Poster

This poster was designed to stir up American workers' support for war after the attack on Pearl Harbor. How successful do you think its appeal for support is?

National Archives

Discussion Questions

1. What persuasive images and slogans are featured in this poster?
2. To what emotions does this poster appeal?
3. Before the attack on Pearl Harbor, the United States was determined to avoid war and remain neutral. In what ways does this poster attempt to change public opinion?

CHAPTER

16

Section 3

LITERATURE SELECTION *from Sophie's Choice*
by William Styron

The main character of this novel is a Polish Catholic woman named Sophie who lives in the United States. This excerpt is a flashback to a time in Poland during World War II when Sophie, her two children, a group of Polish Resistance fighters, and several hundred other Poles are being transported to a concentration camp.

The name Oswiecim—Auschwitz—which had first murmured its way through the compartment made her weak with fear, but she had no doubt whatever that that was where the train was going. A miniscule sliver of light, catching her eye, drew her attention to a tiny crack in the plywood board across the window, and during the first hour of the journey she was able to see enough by the dawn's glow to tell their direction: south. Due south past the country villages that crowd around Warsaw in place of the usual suburban outskirts, due south past greening fields and copses crowded with birch trees, south in the direction of Cracow. Only Auschwitz, of all their plausible destinations, lay south, and she recalled the despair she felt when with her own eyes she verified where they were going. The reputation of Auschwitz was ominous, vile, terrifying. Although in the Gestapo prison rumors had tended to support Auschwitz as the place where they would eventually be shipped, she had hoped incessantly and prayed for a labor camp in Germany, where so many Poles had been transported and where, according to other rumor, conditions were less brutal, less harsh. But as Auschwitz loomed more and more inevitably and now, on the train, made itself inescapable, Sophie was smothered by the realization that she was victim of punishment by association, retribution through chance concurrence. She kept saying to herself: I don't belong here. If she had not had the misfortune of being taken prisoner at the same time as so many of the Home Army members (a stroke of bad luck further complicated by her connection with Wanda, and their common dwelling place, even though she had not lifted a finger to help the Resistance), she might have been adjudged guilty of the serious crime of meat smuggling but not of the infinitely more grave crime of subversion, and hence might not be headed for a destination so forbiddingly malign. But among other ironies, she real-

ized, was this one: she had not been *judged* guilty of anything, merely interrogated and forgotten. She had then been thrown in haphazardly among these partisans, where she was victim less of any specific retributive justice than of a general rage—a kind of berserk lust for complete domination and oppression which seized the Nazis whenever they scored a win over the Resistance, and which this time had even extended to the several hundred bedraggled Poles ensnared in that last savage roundup.

Certain things about the trip she remembered with utter clarity. The stench, the airlessness, the endless shifting of positions—stand up, sit down, stand up again. . . . The view outside the crack, where spring sunlight darkened into drizzling rain. . . . Jan's books, which he tried to read in the feeble light as he sat on her lap: *The Swiss Family Robinson* in German; Polish editions of *White Fang* and *Penrod and Sam.* Eva's two possessions, which she refused to park in the luggage rack but clutched fiercely as if any moment they might be wrested from her hands: the flute in its leather case and her *mis*—the one-eared, one-eyed teddy bear she had kept since the cradle.

More rain outside, a torrent. Now the odor of vomit, pervasive, unextinguishable, cheesy. Fellow passengers: two frightened convent girls of sixteen or so, sobbing, sleeping, waking to murmur prayers to the Holy Virgin; Wiktor, a black-haired, intense, infuriated young Home Army member already plotting revolt or escape, ceaselessly scribbling messages on slips of paper to be passed to Wanda in another compartment; a fear-maddened shriveled old lady claiming to be the niece of Wieniawski, claiming the bundle of parchment she kept pressed close to her to be the original manuscript of his famous *Polonaise,* claiming some kind of immunity, dissolving into tears like the schoolgirls. . . . Hunger pangs beginning. Nothing at all to eat. Another old woman—quite dead—laid out in

> ### She kept saying to herself: I don't belong here.

the exterior aisle on the spot where her heart attack had felled her, her hands frozen around a crucifix and her chalk-white face already smudged by the boots and shoes of people treading over and around her. Through her crevice once more: Cracow at night, the familiar station, moonlit railroad yards where they lay stranded hour after hour. . . . An hour's sleep, then the morning's brightness. Crossing the Vistula, murky and steaming. Two small towns she recognized as the train moved westward through the dusty pollen-gold morning: Skawina, Zator. Eva beginning to cry for the first time, torn by spasms of hunger. Hush, baby. A few more moments' drowse riven by a sun-flooded, splendid, heart-wrenching, manic dream: herself begowned and bediademed, seated at the keyboard before ten thousand onlookers, yet somehow— astoundingly—flying, *flying*, soaring to deliverance on the celestial measures of the Emperor Concerto. Eyelids fluttering apart. A slamming, braking stop. Auschwitz. They waited in the car during most of the rest of the day. At an early moment the generators ceased working; the bulbs went out in the compartment and what remaining light there was cast a milky pallor, filtering through the cracks in the plywood shutters. The distant sound of band music made its way into the compartment. There was a vibration of panic in the car; it was almost palpable, like the prickling of hair all over one's body, and in the near-darkness there came a surge of anxious whispering—hoarse, rising, but as incomprehensible as the rustle of an army of leaves. The convent girls began to wail in unison, beseeching the Holy Mother. Wiktor loudly told them to shut up, while at the same instant Sophie took courage from Wanda's voice, faint from the other end of the car, begging Resistance members and deportees alike to stay calm, stay quiet.

It must have been early in the afternoon when word came regarding the hundreds upon hundreds of Jews from Malkinia in the forward cars. *All Jews in vans* came a note to Wiktor, a note which he read aloud in the gloom and which Sophie, too numb with fright to even clutch Jan and Eva close against her breast for consolation, immediately translated into: All the Jews have gone to the gas. Sophie joined with the convent girls in prayer. It was while she was praying that Eva began to wail loudly. The

children had been brave during the trip, but now the little girl's hunger blossomed into real pain. She squealed in anguish while Sophie tried to rock and soothe her, but nothing seemed to work; the child's screams were for a moment more terrifying to Sophie than the word about the doomed Jews. But soon they stopped. Oddly, it was Jan who came to the rescue. He had a way with his sister and now he took over—at first shushing her in the words of some private language they shared, then pressing next to her with his book. In the pale light he began reading to her from the story of Penrod, about little boys' pranks in the leafy Elysian small-town marrow of America; he was able to laugh and giggle, and his thin soprano singsong cast a gentle spell, combining with Eva's exhaustion to lull her to sleep.

Several hours passed. It was late afternoon. Finally another slip of paper was passed to Wiktor: *AK first car in vans*. This plainly meant one thing—that, like the Jews, the several hundred Home Army members in the car just forward had been transported to Birkenau and the crematoriums. Sophie stared straight ahead, composed her hands in her lap and prepared for death, feeling inexpressible terror but for the first time, too, tasting faintly the blessed bitter relief of acceptance. The old niece of Wieniawski had fallen into a comalike stupor, the *Polonaise* in crumpled disarray, rivulets of drool flowing from the corners of her lips. In trying to reconstruct that moment a long time later, Sophie wondered whether she might not then have become unconscious herself, for the next thing she remembered was her own daylight-dazzled presence outside on the ramp with Jan and Eva, and coming face to face with Hauptsturm-führer Fritz Jemand von Niemand, doctor of medicine. . . .

"Du bist eine Polack," said the doctor. *"Bist du auch eine Kommunistin?"* Sophie placed one arm around Eva's shoulders, the other arm around Jan's waist, saying nothing. The doctor belched, then more sharply elaborated. "I know you're a Polack, but are you also another one of these filthy Communists?" And then in his fog he turned toward the next prisoners, seeming almost to forget Sophie.

Why hadn't she played dumb? *"Nicht sprecht Deutsch."* It could have saved the moment. There was such a press of people. Had she not answered in German he might have let the three of them pass

> *Sophie stared straight ahead, composed her hands in her lap and prepared for death, feeling inexpressible terror.*

through. But there was the cold fact of her terror, and the terror caused her to behave unwisely. She knew now what blind and merciful ignorance had prevented very few Jews who arrived here from knowing, but which her association with Wanda and the others had caused her to know and to dread with fear beyond utterance: a selection. She and the children were undergoing at this very moment the ordeal she had heard about—rumored in Warsaw a score of times in whispers—but which had seemed at once so unbearable and unlikely to happen to her that she had thrust it out of her mind. But here she was, and here was the doctor. While over there—just beyond the roofs of the boxcars recently vacated by the death-bound Malkinia Jews—was Birkenau, and the doctor could select for its abyssal doors anyone whom he desired. This thought caused her such terror that instead of keeping her mouth shut she said, *"Ich bin polnisch! In Krakow geboren!"* Then she blurted helplessly, "I'm not Jewish! Or my children—they're not Jewish either." And added, "They are racially pure. They speak German." Finally she announced, "I'm a Christian. I'm a devout Catholic. . . ."

The doctor was a little unsteady on his feet. He leaned over for a moment to an enlisted underling with a clipboard and murmured something, meanwhile absorbedly picking his nose. Eva, pressing heavily against Sophie's legs, began to cry. "So you believe in Christ the Redeemer?" the doctor said in a thick-tongued but oddly abstract voice, like that of a lecturer examining the delicately shaded facet of a proposition in logic. Then he said something which for an instant was totally mystifying: "Did He not say, 'Suffer the little children to come unto Me'?" He turned back to her, moving with the twitchy methodicalness of a drunk.

Sophie, with an inanity poised on her tongue and choked with fear, was about to attempt a reply when the doctor said, "You may keep one of your children."

"Bitte?" said Sophie.

"You may keep one of your children," he repeated. "The other one will have to go. Which one will you keep?"

"You mean, I have to choose?"

"You're a Polack, not a Yid. That gives you a privilege—a choice."

Her thought processes dwindled, ceased. Then

> *"Don't make me choose," she heard herself plead in a whispher, "I can't choose."*

she felt her legs crumple. "I can't choose! I can't choose!" She began to scream. Oh, how she recalled her own screams! Tormented angels never screeched so loudly above hell's pandemonium. *"Ich kann nicht wahlen!"* she screamed.

The doctor was aware of unwanted attention. "Shut up!" he ordered. "Hurry now and choose. Choose, . . . or I'll send them both over there. Quick!"

She could not believe any of this. She could not believe that she was now kneeling on the hurtful, abrading concrete, drawing her children toward her so smotheringly tight that she felt that their flesh might be engrafted to hers even through layers of clothes. Her disbelief was total, deranged. It was disbelief reflected in the eyes of the gaunt, waxy-skinned young Rottenfuhrer, the doctor's aide, to whom she inexplicably found herself looking upward in supplication. He appeared stunned, and he returned her gaze with a wide-eyed baffled expression, as if to say: I can't understand this either.

"Don't make me choose," she heard herself plead in a whisper, "I can't choose."

"Send them both over there, then," the doctor said to the aide, *"nach links."*

"Mama!" She heard Eva's thin but soaring cry at the instant that she thrust the child away from her and rose from the concrete with a clumsy stumbling motion. "Take the baby!" she called out. "Take my little girl!"

At this point the aide—with a careful gentleness that Sophie would try without success to forget—tugged at Eva's hand and led her away into the waiting legion of the damned. She would forever retain a dim impression that the child had continued to look back, beseeching. But because she was now almost completely blinded by salty, thick, copious tears she was spared whatever expression Eva wore, and she was always grateful for that. For in the bleakest honesty of her heart she knew that she would never have been able to tolerate it, driven nearly mad as she was by her last glimpse of that vanishing small form.

Discussion Questions

1. Why was Sophie sent to Auschwitz?
2. What choice did the doctor force Sophie to make?
3. Given the circumstances, do you agree with Sophie's actions? Why or why not?

CHAPTER 16

Section 3

AMERICAN LIVES Elie Wiesel

Dedicated to Memory and to Humanity

"I have tried to keep memory alive. I have tried to fight those who would forget. Because if we forget, we are accomplices. . . . Our lives no longer belong to us alone; they belong to all those who need us desperately."—Elie Wiesel, Nobel Peace Prize acceptance speech (1986)

When he accepted the 1986 Nobel Peace Prize, Elie Wiesel spoke of his life's work. As a survivor of the Holocaust, Wiesel felt that he bore a special duty. For more than four decades, he has devoted his life to remembering those who died in the Nazi death camps. Through his writings, speeches, and actions, he has tried to ensure that the world will never forget them. He has toiled with equal dedication to prevent any group anywhere in the world from suffering at the hands of others.

Born in 1928 in Romania, Wiesel was raised in the traditions of Hasidic Judaism. This faith stressed emotional belief. Its principles were embodied in collections of stories. Hearing these stories from his father and grandfather, Wiesel developed a strong faith and a love for the traditions. His life, with his parents and three sisters, was peaceful.

That peace was shattered in the 1940s. Word filtered from the outside that Nazi Germany was persecuting Jews. Many—even Wiesel's father—refused to believe the stories. However, in 1944 the truth became painfully clear. The Nazis entered Wiesel's village to deport all Jews. Wiesel, his parents, and his three sisters were taken to Birkenau in Poland, the first of two Nazi death camps where Wiesel was to be held for the next year.

Wiesel's parents and youngest sister did not survive the camps, though at the time Wiesel knew for certain only of the death of his father. After his liberation by the U.S. Army in April of 1945, Wiesel reached Paris, where a news photographer took a photo of him and other survivors arriving in the city. It appeared in a magazine, which happened to be seen by one of Wiesel's two older sisters. By this accident, they learned of the survival of each other.

To make a living, Wiesel became a journalist, and, while working, he studied philosophy in Paris and India. After his liberation in 1945, Wiesel had vowed to wait ten years before writing about the Holocaust. Finally the time passed, and in 1956 he published a memoir in Yiddish titled *And the*

World Was Silent. Four years later an abbreviated form of the book was published in English as an autobiographical novel, *Night*. The book gave a searing account of life in a Nazi death camp and the guilt of having survived the conditions.

With this book, Wiesel began his life's work. In novels, stories, plays, and essays, he retold stories from the Bible or Hasidic tradition or explored the spiritual crisis caused by the Holocaust. His early works were dark and despairing, but as time passed, Wiesel wrote of hope. "Just as despair can come to one only from other human beings," he once said, "hope, too, can be given to one only by other human beings." By this time he had made his home in New York City and became a U.S. citizen in 1963. He taught at universities and lectured all over the world. In New York, listeners packed his yearly lectures on Jewish tradition.

He places great faith in the power of writing. "Words could sometimes, in moments of grace, attain the quality of deeds." At the same time, Wiesel puts his ideas into action. In the 1960s he traveled to the Soviet Union. This trip spurred him to write a novel and a play protesting the persecution of Jewish people there. He has campaigned for human rights, traveling to Cambodia, South Africa, and Bangladesh as well as other strife-torn lands of the 1970s and 1980s. Among his awards, besides the Nobel Peace Prize of 1986, are the Presidential Medal of Honor (1992) and the Interfaith Council on the Holocaust Humanitarian Award (1994).

Questions

1. What does Wiesel mean by saying that "if we forget, we are accomplices"?
2. One critic called Wiesel "part conscience . . . and part warning signal." How is that appropriate?
3. Do you agree or disagree with Wiesel's statement that words "can attain the quality of deeds"? Explain.

CHAPTER
16
Section 4

AMERICAN LIVES Charles A. Lindbergh
Private Man, Public Figure

"We must not be misguided by this foreign propaganda that our frontiers lie in Europe. What more could we ask than the Atlantic Ocean on the east, the Pacific on the west? An ocean is a formidable barrier, even for modern aircraft."
— *Charles A. Lindbergh, radio speech (1939)*

Charles A. Lindbergh (1902–1974) was a private man whose daring flight in 1927 made him a public figure. However, fame brought personal tragedy, and his popularity declined when he spoke against U.S. involvement in World War II.

Lindbergh became a stunt pilot in his early twenties and soon joined the army, graduating first in his flight class. By 1926 he was flying for the new airmail service from Chicago to St. Louis.

Then he went after a big prize—a long-standing offer by a French hotel manager in New York to pay $25,000 to anyone who could fly alone, nonstop, from the United States to Paris or vice versa—a 3,600-mile dare. Lindbergh found some backers and began customizing a plane. The plane, named the *Spirit of St. Louis*, was finished in San Diego in 1927, and he flew it across the country with a stopover in St. Louis. His 22 hours of flying time set a new cross-country record. Ten days after leaving San Diego, Lindbergh flew east from Long Island, out over the Atlantic Ocean. Alone in a stripped-down plane for thirty-three-and-a-half hours, he finally landed in Paris. Thousands cheered his arrival. Back in the United States, he was given a parade in New York City, where 4 million cheered his feat.

Lindbergh became America's goodwill ambassador to the world. He married in 1929, and his wife learned to be a pilot. Together, they flew all over the world. All the time, Lindbergh tested technical improvements to planes.

Then, in 1932, tragedy struck. The Lindberghs' infant son was kidnapped from their home. A note asked for $50,000 in ransom money. Two-and-a-half months later, the baby was found, dead. The Lindberghs were grief-stricken, and the nation mourned with them. A suspect was finally tried and convicted, but press coverage of the tragedy had left the Lindberghs totally without privacy. In 1936, they left the United States for England.

They lived there for the next three years, taking a number of trips to the continent. On several occasions, they were hosted by Hermann Goering,

the leader of the air force of Nazi Germany. Impressed by its size, Lindbergh warned officials in other countries of the Nazis' growing air power. On one visit to Germany, Goering surprised him by giving him a medal. Lindbergh was widely criticized for accepting it.

In 1939, Lindbergh returned to the United States. Certain that war in Europe would break out soon, he was determined to work to prevent U.S. involvement. (His father had served in the House of Representatives from 1907–1917, where he had opposed U.S. entry into World War I.) Germany, Lindbergh said, was too strong. Britain was an unreliable ally. At the same time, he urged Americans to strengthen the nation's defenses—especially by adding 10,000 war planes. Still a member of the army reserve, he resigned his commission early in 1941 and joined the America First Committee. He spoke at countless rallies. Then in September of 1941, he went so far as to blame Roosevelt, the British, and Jewish people for pushing the country to war. Lindbergh denied that he was prejudiced, but the charge of anti-Semitism stuck. No longer a credible speaker, he left the committee.

When the Japanese attacked Pearl Harbor in December, Lindbergh joined the calls to unite the nation, but he was not allowed to re-enter the army. Still, he contributed advice—and some test flying—to the effort to improve military aircraft. After the war, he was busy in the airline industry and later was an advisor to the government's space program. His autobiography, *The Spirit of St. Louis* (1954), won a Pulitzer Prize and was filmed in 1957.

Questions

1. What did Lindbergh lose in gaining fame?
2. Based on the opening quotation, why did Lindbergh think that the United States should not become involved in World War II?
3. Why did Lindbergh withdraw from the America First committee?

GUIDED READING *Mobilizing for Defense*

CHAPTER 17
Section 1

A. As you read about how the United States mobilized for war, note how each of the following contributed to that effort.

1. Selective Service System	6. Office of Scientific Research and Development (OSRD)
2. Women	7. Entertainment industry
3. Minorities	8. Office of Price Administration (OPA)
4. Manufacturers	9. War Production Board (WPB)
5. A. Philip Randolph	10. Rationing

B. On the back of this paper, briefly describe **George Marshall**'s position on how women could contribute to the war effort. Then, explain who the **Nisei** were and what happened to them.

GUIDED READING *The War for Europe and*
North Africa

A. As you read about the Allied war effort, take notes to explain what made each
event a critical moment or turning point in the war.

February 1943	End of Battle of Stalingrad	→	1.
May 1943	End of Operation Torch	→	2.
Mid- 1943	Victory in Battle of the Atlantic	→	3.
June 1944	D-Day	→	4.
July 1944	Liberation of Majdanek	→	5.
August 1944	Liberation of France	→	6.
October 1944	Capture of Aachen	→	7.
January 1945	End of Battle of the Bulge	→	8.
Spring 1945	End of Italian campaign	→	9.
May 1945	V-E Day	→	10.

B. On the back of this paper, note the official title of each of the following and
describe the roles they played during the war.

Dwight D. Eisenhower   **George Patton**   **Harry S. Truman**

Name _____ Date _____

CHAPTER

17

Section 3

GUIDED READING *The War in the Pacific*

A. As you read about the defeat of Japan and the end of the war, write notes to
describe important wartime and war-related events. (Leave the shaded box blank.)

The War in the Pacific		
Date and Place	**Leaders Involved**	**What happened?**
1. April 1942, Bataan		
2. June 1942, Midway		
3. August 1942, Guadalcanal		
4. October 1944, Leyte Gulf		
5. March 1945, Iwo Jima		
6. June 1945, Okinawa		
7. September 1945, Tokyo Bay		

The Science of War		
Date and Place	**Leaders Involved**	**What happened?**
8. July 1945, Los Alamos		
9. August 1945, Hiroshima, Nagasaki		

Planning and Rebuilding for Peace		
Date and Place	**Leaders Involved**	**What happened?**
10. February 1945, Yalta		
11. April 1945, San Francisco		
12. 1945–1949, Nuremberg		

B. On the back of this paper, explain or define **kamikaze** and **Manhattan Project.**

CHAPTER

17

Section 4

GUIDED READING *The Home Front*

A. As you read this section, write notes to answer questions about the impact of the
war on various segments of American society.

How did the war and its immediate aftermath affect the following?	
1. Labor	2. Agriculture
3. Population centers	4. Family life
5. Returning GIs	

How did these groups react to discrimination and racism during and after the war?
6. African Americans
7. Mexican Americans
8. Japanese Americans

B. On the back of this paper, briefly explain why **James Farmer** is an important
historical figure.

BUILDING VOCABULARY *The United States in World War II*

A. Multiple Choice Circle the letter before the term or name that best completes the sentence.

1. The civil rights leader who battled discrimination in war-related jobs was (a) George Marshall (b) A. Philip Randolph (c) Henry J. Kaiser.

2. The Allied invasion of France to free western Europe from the Nazis was known as (a) D-Day (b) V-E Day (c) the Battle of the Bulge.

3. The commander of U.S. forces in Europe was (a) Omar Bradley (b) George Patton (c) Dwight D. Eisenhower.

4. The first atomic bomb used against Japan was dropped on (a) Nagasaki (b) Hiroshima (c) Iwo Jima.

5. The GI Bill of Rights provided help to (a) widows of fallen servicemen (b) worn-torn countries of Europe (c) returning veterans.

B. Evaluating Write *T* in the blank if the statement is true. If the statement is false, write *F* in the blank and then write the corrected statement on the line below.

_____ 1. James Farmer was instrumental in the formation of the Women's Auxiliary Army Corps.

_____

_____ 2. The Battle of Midway was considered a turning point in the battle against the Nazis.

_____

_____ 3. Scientist J. Robert Oppenheimer led the effort to develop the first atomic bomb.

_____

_____ 4. Upon Franklin Roosevelt's death, his vice-president, Harry Truman, became president.

_____

_____ 5. The Manhattan Project was the code name of a plot to assassinate Adolf Hitler.

_____

C. Writing Write a paragraph about the discrimination faced by minorities during World War II using the following terms.

James Farmer   **Congress of Racial Equality (CORE)**   **internment**

SKILLBUILDER PRACTICE *Analyzing Assumptions and Biases*

CHAPTER 17

Section 1

During World War II, many companies used their advertisements not only to sell their products but also to encourage patriotism and support for the American way of life. Read this text of a 1944 magazine ad created by a sporting goods company. Then fill in the chart with evidence of bias toward the American way of life. (See Skillbuilder Handbook, p. R15.)

Backbone . . . not Wishbone!

If the Pilgrims and their loyal women folk had had wabbly *wish*bones in place of their sturdy backbones; if the backbones of the patriots at Valley Forge had been wishy-washy—America, land of the free today, *would* have ended in wishful thinking.

But the men who discovered, dreamed, worked and fought to build our great democracy, put their own steely courage into the backbone of this nation. It is backbone that *shows* whenever the chips are down.

You see it in our modern industrial marvels that began in a little iron-founder's shop less than two centuries ago.

You see it in our scientific miracles—in our agricultural achievements—and in our mighty war effort, today.

Have you considered that the maintenance of America's superb backbone lies in our matchless

*youth*power? It does.

Out there on the playfields of our great democratic nation, where our youth—our potential manpower—fight to the last ditch in friendly fierceness, for a coveted goal—in vigorous man-to-man, competitive sports—the *backbone* of our *nation* is renewed and stiffened.

On these battlefields of competitive play our boys and our girls, too, learn initiative, courage, determination, fighting spirit, will-to-win despite all odds, tempered with fair play.

And on these fields is inculcated into their minds and hearts an unrealized appreciation of what it means to live in a *free* America. Try to take this freedom of theirs away from them—this personal privilege to think and dream and do in freedom—to be oneself—to fight for a goal and win it—and that realization becomes a living flame. And in this fact is our greatest guarantee that America will continue to be the land of the free.

from *Life* (September 11, 1944).

Words that indicate strong positive feelings	
Words that indicate negative feelings	
Idealized descriptions and images	

CHAPTER
17
Section 1

RETEACHING ACTIVITY *Mobilizing for Defense*

Completion

A. Complete each sentence with the appropriate term or name.

atomic bomb   inflation
women   African Americans
unemployment   rationing
Asian Americans   Mexican Americans

1. While segregated and limited largely to noncombat roles, about one million _____ served in the U.S. military during the war.

2. By 1944, _____ made up about a third of all workers laboring in war-related industries.

3. The Office of Price Administration tried to fight _____ by freezing prices on most goods.

4. The most significant development of the Office of Scientific Research and Development was the _____.

5. Many average Americans contributed to the war effort by engaging in _____.

Main Ideas

B. Answer the following questions in the space provided.

1. In what ways did members of the Women's Auxiliary Corps contribute to the war effort?

_____

_____

2. In what way did American industries contribute to the war?

_____

_____

3. In what ways did the federal government take control of the economy during the war?

_____

_____

CHAPTER
17
Section 2

RETEACHING ACTIVITY *The War for Europe*
and North Africa

Sequencing

A. Put the events below in the correct chronological order.

_____ 1. Germany surrenders.

_____ 2. Benito Mussolini falls from power.

_____ 3. Germans lose last-ditch effort at Battle of the Bulge.

_____ 4. Soviets repel the Nazis in the Battle of Stalingrad.

_____ 5. Allies begin liberation of Europe with D-Day invasion.

_____ 6. Allies gain control of North Africa.

Evaluating

B. Write *T* in the blank if the statement is true. If the statement is false, write *F* in the blank and then write the corrected statement on the line below.

_____ 1. Upon Germany's surrender, Adolf Hitler was tried before an international court for his war crimes.

_____

_____ 2. D-Day was the largest land-sea-air operation in army history.

_____

_____ 3. The Tuskegee Airmen was a squadron of all-black pilots who performed heroically during the fighting in Italy.

_____

_____ 4. The leader of Germany Afrika Korps was the Karl Doenitz, the legendary Desert Fox.

_____

_____ 5. The Allies suffered many early defeats before eventually winning the battle for supremacy of the Atlantic Ocean.

_____

CHAPTER 17

Section 3

RETEACHING ACTIVITY *The War in the Pacific*

Reading Comprehension

_____ 1. After scoring numerous victories throughout the Pacific, the Japanese navy was finally turned back at the
   a. Battle of the Bulge.
   b. Battle of the Coral Sea.
   c. Battle of Midway.
   d. Battle of Leyete Gulf.

_____ 2. The island on which nearly 8,000 U.S. soldiers and some 110,000 Japanese soldiers lost their lives was
   a. Iwo Jima.
   b. the Philippines.
   c. Okinawa.
   d. Midway.

_____ 3. The Japanese finally surrendered after the United States dropped a second atomic bomb on
   a. Nagasaki.
   b. Hiroshima.
   c. Tokyo.
   d. Okinawa.

_____ 4. The Nuremburg Trials sought to punish for war crimes mainly the leader of
   a. Germany.
   b. Japan.
   c. Italy.
   d. the Soviet Union.

_____ 5. The Yalta Conference to discuss the fate of the post war world brought together the leaders of the United States, Great Britain, and
   a. France.
   b. China.
   c. Spain.
   d. the Soviet Union.

_____ 6. In the wake of its defeat, Japan was occupied and rebuilt by forces from
   a. China.
   b. France.
   c. Great Britain.
   d. the United States.

CHAPTER
17
Section 4

RETEACHING ACTIVITY *The Home Front*

Finding Main Ideas

The following questions deal with events on the home front during World War II.
Answer them in the space provided.

1. What significant population shifts occurred during the war?

_____

_____

2. How did the GI Bill of Rights help war veterans?

_____

_____

3. What was the goal of the Congress of Racial Equality?

_____

_____

4. What were the zoot-suit riots?

_____

_____

5. What discrimination did Japanese Americans face during the war?

_____

_____

6. What did the Supreme Court decide in *Korematsu* v. *United States*?

_____

_____

CHAPTER 17

Section 2

GEOGRAPHY APPLICATION: PLACE *Thunderclap*

Directions: Read the paragraphs below and study the map carefully. Then answer the questions that follow.

One of the most controversial incidents of World War II was the Allied aerial bombing of Dresden late in the war. Located in eastern Germany near the Polish and Czech borders, Dresden was, according to writer Alexander McKee, a city with "fantastic architecture," with a town center "housing world-class collections of paintings, statues, and art objects of all kinds."

By means of a plan code-named Thunderclap, the Allies sought to deliver to Germany a "mighty blow"—the destruction of a major city to hasten Germany's surrender in a war it had no chance of winning. Eventually, Dresden was selected. The city's numerous military targets included an infantry barracks, an autobahn (expressway) skirting the city to the west and leading to the German front, a railway network, bridges, and a number of factories.

During massive night and day bombings by Allied aircraft between February 13 and 15, 1945, the heart of Dresden was almost completely destroyed. The bombing was so intense during one raid that the explosions created a firestorm in which thousands of people were suffocated as the fires consumed all the oxygen for blocks around. Estimates of the number of people killed in the raids range from 25,000 to 135,000. The exact figure will never be known, because at the time Dresden was teeming with thousands of refugees from other German cities.

Although some targets such as the autobahn were left intact, the physical damage was staggering. Out of 220,000 living units—houses and apartments—more than 90,000 were destroyed or made uninhabitable by the bombing.

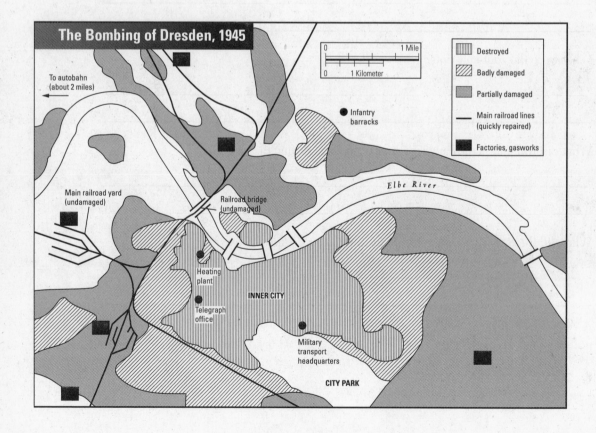

The Bombing of Dresden, 1945

0   1 Mile
0   1 Kilometer

Destroyed
Badly damaged
Partially damaged
Main railroad lines (quickly repaired)
Factories, gasworks

To autobahn (about 2 miles)

Infantry barracks

Elbe River

Main railroad yard (undamaged)

Railroad bridge (undamaged)

Heating plant

INNER CITY

Telegraph office

Military transport headquarters

CITY PARK

Interpreting Text and Visuals

1. What is the purpose of the map? _____

_____

2. What part of Dresden was most heavily damaged? _____

3. What places in and around Dresden might the Allies have considered targets of
   military significance? _____

_____

_____

4. Which of these targets was completely destroyed? _____

_____

5. In what parts of Dresden were most of these targets located? _____

6. On the basis of the map, what might you conclude about the purpose of
   Thunderclap? _____

_____

_____

7. Sir Arthur Harris, British commander of the Allied raids, wrote after the raids that
   "Dresden was a mass of munitions [guns and ammunition] works, an intact
   government center, and a key transportation center to the East. It is now none of
   those things." To what extent do you agree or disagree with the statement? Why?

_____

_____

_____

_____

8. Why do you think the bombing of Dresden is controversial? _____

_____

_____

_____

OUTLINE MAP *Crisis in Europe*

CHAPTER 17

Section 2

A. Review the map "World War II: Europe and Africa, 1942–1944" on page 572 of your textbook. Then, on the accompanying outline map, label the following bodies of water and countries. (You may abbreviate country names where necessary.) Finally, color or shade the map to distinguish the regions identified in the key.

Bodies of Water	Countries		
Atlantic Ocean	Great Britain	Saudi Arabia	Portugal
North Sea	Germany	Italy	Spain
Mediterranean Sea	Poland	Turkey	Switzerland
Black Sea	France	Soviet Union	Norway
	Egypt	Czechoslovakia	Sweden
	Syria	Austria	Finland
	Iraq	Hungary	Denmark

B. After completing the map, use it to answer the following questions.

1. Which two major Allied nations appear on the map? _____

_____

2. Which of the countries you labeled remained neutral in 1942? _____

_____

3. How would you describe the Axis's situation in Europe at the time represented
   by the map? _____

_____

_____

4. Think about U.S. participation in the war in Europe. How might the Axis have
   benefited by gaining control of Great Britain by 1942? _____

_____

_____

5. By June 1943, the Allies had regained control of North Africa. What was the
   advantage of controlling this region? _____

_____

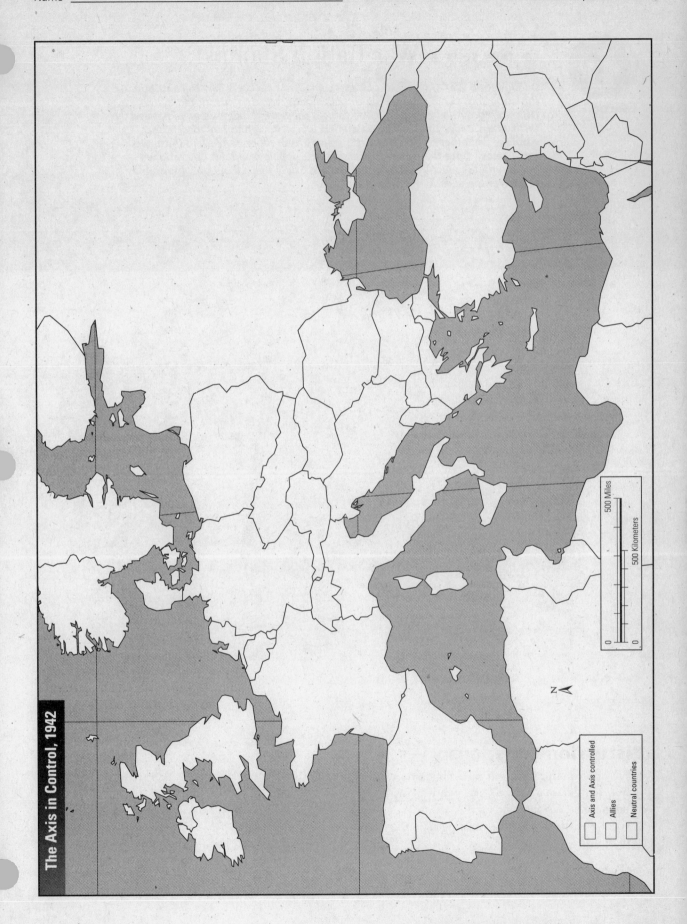

The Axis in Control, 1942

500 Miles

500 Kilometers

N

Axis and Axis controlled

Allies

Neutral countries

CHAPTER 17

Section 1

PRIMARY SOURCE War Ration Stamps

During World War II, Americans on the home front did their part to contribute to the war effort. For example, they complied with rationing introduced by the Office of Price Administration (OPA) to help conserve goods that were needed by the military. Under this system, consumers were allowed to buy meat, sugar, gasoline, and other scarce items with stamps from ration books like those pictured below. Once they used up their stamps, people could not buy rationed goods until they received additional stamps. Study the ration book and stamps to answer the questions below.

The Granger Collection, New York.

Discussion Questions

1. Why do you think the war ration book requires information on a person's age, sex, weight, height, and occupation?

2. What was the penalty for violating rationing regulations?

3. Most Americans during World War II accepted rationing. Why do you think this was so?

CHAPTER 17

Section 2

PRIMARY SOURCE War Dispatch from Ernie Pyle

Journalist Ernie Pyle accompanied American soldiers to the Pacific, Europe, England, and North Africa to offer a "worm's-eye-view" of World War II. He was killed by a Japanese sniper's bullet on Ie Shima in 1945. As you read this excerpt from one of Pyle's popular columns, think about his attitudes toward the infantry

IN THE FRONT LINES BEFORE MATEUR, NORTHERN TUNISIA, May 2, 1943—We're now with an infantry outfit that has battled ceaselessly for four days and nights. . . .

I love the infantry because they are the underdogs. They are the mud-rain-frost-and-wind boys. They have no comforts, and they even learn to live without the necessities. And in the end they are the guys that wars can't be won without.

I wish you could see just one of the ineradicable pictures I have in my mind today. In this particular picture I am sitting among clumps of sword-grass on a steep and rocky hillside that we have just taken. We are looking out over a vast rolling country to the rear.

A narrow path comes like a ribbon over a hill miles away, down a long slope, across a creek, up a slope and over another hill.

All along the length of this ribbon there is now a thin line of men. For four days and nights they have fought hard, eaten little, washed none, and slept hardly at all. Their nights have been violent with attack, fright, butchery, and their days sleepless and miserable with the crash of artillery.

The men are walking. They are fifty feet apart, for dispersal. Their walk is slow, for they are dead weary, as you can tell even when looking at them from behind. Every line and sag of their bodies speaks their inhuman exhaustion.

On their shoulders and backs they carry heavy steel tripods, machine-gun barrels, leaden boxes of ammunition. Their feet seem to sink into the ground from the overload they are bearing.

They don't slouch. It is the terrible deliberation of each step that spells out their appalling tiredness. Their faces are black and unshaven. They are young men, but the grime and whiskers and exhaustion make them look middle-aged.

In their eyes as they pass is not hatred, not excitement, not despair, not the tonic of their victory—there is just the simple expression of being here as though they had been here doing this forever, and nothing else.

The line moves on, but it never ends. All afternoon men keep coming round the hill and vanishing eventually over the horizon. It is one long tired line of antlike men.

There is an agony in your heart and you almost feel ashamed to look at them. They are just guys from Broadway and Main Street, but you wouldn't remember them. They are too far away now. They are too tired. Their world can never be known to you, but if you could see them just once, just for an instant, you would know that no matter how hard people work back home they are not keeping pace with these infantrymen in Tunisia.

from David Nichols, ed., *Ernie's War: The Best of Ernie Pyle's World War II Dispatches* (New York: Random House, 1986), 112–113.

Activity Options

1. Write a letter home in the voice of a World War II soldier. Draw on details in this excerpt from Pyle's column as well as information in your textbook to bring the realities of being in an infantry outfit to life.

2. Work with a partner to interview a World War II veteran—a family member, a neighbor, or a person who lives in your community—about his experiences in the military. Then compare your interview subject's impressions with those of Ernie Pyle.

3. Find photographs of American soldiers in the infantry that might have accompanied Pyle's column. Then work with your classmates to create a World War II photo essay.

CHAPTER 17

Section 3

PRIMARY SOURCE The Bombing of Nagasaki

On August 6, 1945, the United States dropped an atomic bomb on Hiroshima, Japan. When Japan's leaders did not surrender at once, a second bomb was dropped over Nagasaki three days later. Notice the descriptive details that New York Times reporter William L. Laurence used to report the bombing.

We flew southward down the channel and at 11:33 crossed the coastline and headed straight for Nagasaki, about one hundred miles to the west. Here again we circled until we found an opening in the clouds. It was 12:01 and the goal of our mission had arrived.

We heard the prearranged signal on our radio, put on our arc welder's glasses, and watched tensely the maneuverings of the strike ship about half a mile in front of us.

"There she goes!" someone said.

Out of the belly of *The Great Artiste* what looked like a black object went downward.

Captain Bock swung around to get out of range; but even though we were turning away in the opposite direction, and despite the fact that it was broad daylight in our cabin, all of us became aware of a giant flash that broke through the dark barrier of our arc welder's lenses and flooded our cabin with intense light.

We removed our glasses after the first flash, but the light still lingered on, a bluish-green light that illuminated the entire sky all around. A tremendous blast wave struck our ship and made it tremble from nose to tail. This was followed by four more blasts in rapid succession, each resounding like the boom of cannon fire hitting our plane from all directions.

Observers in the tail of our ship saw a giant ball of fire rise as though from the bowels of the earth, belching forth enormous white smoke rings. Next they saw a giant pillar of purple fire, ten thousand feet high, shooting skyward with enormous speed.

By the time our ship had made another turn in the direction of the atomic explosion the pillar of purple fire had reached the level of our altitude. Only about forty-five seconds had passed. Awestruck, we watched it shoot upward like a meteor coming from the earth instead of from outer space, becoming ever more alive as it climbed skyward through the white clouds. It was no longer smoke, or dust, or even a cloud of fire. It was a living thing, a new species of being, born right before our incredulous eyes.

At one stage of its evolution, covering millions of years in terms of seconds, the entity assumed the form of a giant square totem pole, with its base about three miles long, tapering off to about a mile at the top. Its bottom was brown, its center was amber, its top white. But it was a living totem pole, carved with many grotesque masks grimacing at the earth.

Then, just when it appeared as though the thing had settled down into a state of permanence, there came shooting out of the top a giant mushroom that increased the height of the pillar to a total of forty-five thousand feet. The mushroom top was even more alive than the pillar, seething and boiling in a white fury of creamy foam, sizzling upward and then descending earthward, a thousand Old Faithful geysers rolled into one.

It kept struggling in an elemental fury, like a creature in the act of breaking the bonds that held it down. In a few seconds it had freed itself from its gigantic stem and floated upward with tremendous speed, its momentum carrying it into the stratosphere to a height of about sixty thousand feet.

But no sooner did this happen when another mushroom, smaller in size than the first one, began emerging out of the pillar. It was as though the decapitated monster was growing a new head.

from *New York Times,* September 9, 1945. Reprinted in Richard B. Morris and James Woodress, eds., *Voices from America's Past,* vol. 3, The Twentieth Century (New York: Dutton, 1962), 161–163.

Research Options

1. Find out more about the bombing of Hiroshima and Nagasaki. How many people were killed by the bomb blasts? How many were injured?
2. Use on-line or print resources to research the debate in 1945 among scientists and government officials over whether the atomic bomb should be used on Japan. Then, with your classmates, hold a debate in which you argue for or against using the bomb.

CHAPTER 17

Section 4

PRIMARY SOURCE *from Farewell to Manzanar*

During World War II, seven-year-old Jeanne Wakatsuki was sent to Manzanar, a Japanese-American internment camp in Owens Valley, California. As you read this excerpt from her memoir, think about her first impressions of the camp.

We rode all day. By the time we reached our destination, the shades were up. It was late afternoon. The first thing I saw was a yellow swirl across a blurred, reddish setting sun. The bus was being pelted by what sounded like splattering rain. It wasn't rain. This was my first look at something I would soon know very well, a billowing flurry of dust and sand churned up by the wind through Owens Valley.

We drove past a barbed-wire fence, through a gate, and into an open space where trunks and sacks and packages had been dumped from the baggage trucks that drove out ahead of us. I could see a few tents set up, the first rows of black barracks, and beyond them blurred by sand, rows of barracks that seemed to spread for miles across this plain. People were sitting on cartons or milling around, with their backs to the wind, waiting to see which friends or relatives might be on this bus. As we approached, they turned or stood up, and some moved toward us expectantly. But inside the bus no one stirred. No one waved or spoke. They just stared out of the windows, ominously silent. I didn't understand this. Hadn't we finally arrived, our whole family intact? I opened a window, leaned out, and yelled happily. "Hey! This whole bus is full of Wakatsukis!"

Outside, the greeters smiled. Inside there was an explosion of laughter, hysterical, tension-breaking laughter that left my brothers choking and whacking each other across the shoulders.

We had pulled up just in time for dinner. The mess halls weren't completed yet. An outdoor chow line snaked around a half-finished building that broke a good part of the wind. They issued us army mess kits, the round metal kind that fold over, and plopped in scoops of canned Vienna sausage, canned string beans, steamed rice that had been cooked too long, and on top of the rice a serving of canned apricots. The Caucasian servers were thinking that the fruit poured over rice would make a good dessert. Among the Japanese, of course, rice is never eaten with sweet foods, only with salty or savory foods. Few of us could eat such a mixture.

But at this point no one dared protest. It would have been impolite. I was horrified when I saw the apricot syrup seeping through my little mound of rice. I opened my mouth to complain. My mother jabbed me in the back to keep quiet. We moved on through the line and joined the others squatting in the lee of half-raised walls, dabbing courteously at what was, for almost everyone there, an inedible concoction.

After dinner we were taken to Block 16, a cluster of fifteen barracks that had just been finished a day or so earlier—although finished was hardly the word for it. The shacks were built of one thickness of pine planking covered with tarpaper. They sat on concrete footings, with about two feet of open space between the floorboards and the ground. Gaps showed between the planks, and as the weeks passed and the green wood dried out, the gaps widened. Knotholes gaped in the uncovered floor.

Each barracks was divided into six units, sixteen by twenty feet, about the size of a living room, with one bare bulb hanging from the ceiling and an oil stove for heat. We were assigned two of these for the twelve people in our family group; and our official family "number" was enlarged by three digits—16 plus the number of this barracks. We were issued steel army cots, two brown army blankets each, and some mattress covers, which my brothers stuffed with straw.

from Jeanne Wakatsuki Houston and James D. Houston, *Farewell to Manzanar* (New York: Bantam Books, 1973), 14–15.

Discussion Questions

1. What were living accommodations like in the camp?
2. Why do you think the accommodations at Manzanar were so stark and crowded?
3. What incident from this excerpt demonstrates a lack of cultural awareness on the part of those running the camp?

CHAPTER 17

Section 4

LITERATURE SELECTION *from* **Snow Falling on Cedars**
by David Guterson

This excerpt from Snow Falling on Cedars *tells what happens to Japanese Americans living on San Piedro, an island off the coast of Washington, after the bombing of Pearl Harbor. As you read, think about the difficulties that Japanese Americans like Fujiko and her daughters faced as a result of relocation.*

The problem was resolved for them on March 21 when the U. S. War Relocation Authority announced that islanders of Japanese descent had eight days to prepare to leave.

The Kobayashis—they'd planted a thousand dollars' worth of rhubarb on five acres in Center Valley—negotiated an agreement with Torval Rasmussen to tend and harvest their crop. The Masuis weeded their strawberry fields and worked at staking peas in the moonlight; they wanted to leave things in good condition for Michael Burns and his ne'er-do-well brother Patrick, who'd agreed to take care of their farm. The Sumidas decided to sell at cut-rate and close their nursery down; on Thursday and Friday they held all-day sales and watched pruning tools, fertilizer, cedar chairs, birdbaths, garden benches, paper lanterns, fountain cats, tree wrap, caddies, and bonsai trees go out the door with whoever was willing to take them. On Sunday they put padlocks on the greenhouse doors and asked Piers Petersen to keep an eye on things. They gave Piers their flock of laying chickens as well as a pair of mallard ducks.

Len Kato and Johnny Kobashigawa traveled island roads in a three-ton haying truck hauling loads of furniture, packing crates, and appliances to the Japanese Community Center hall. Filled to the rafters with beds, sofas, stoves, refrigerators, chests of drawers, desks, tables, and chairs, the hall was locked and boarded up at six P.M. on Sunday evening. Three retired gill-netters—Gillon Crichton, Sam Goodall, and Eric Hoffman, Sr.— were sworn in as deputies by San Piedro's sheriff for the purpose of guarding its contents.

The War Relocation Authority moved into musty offices at the old W. W. Beason Cannery dock, just outside Amity Harbor. The dock housed not only the Army Transport Command but representatives of the Farm Security Administration and the Federal Employment Service. Kaspars Hinkle, who coached the high school baseball team, stormed into the war relocation office on a late Thursday afternoon—everyone was just then preparing to leave—and slammed his roster on the secretary's desk: his starting catcher, second baseman, and two outfielders, he said—not to mention his two best pitchers—were going to miss the whole season. Couldn't this matter be thought through again? None of these kids were spies!

On Saturday evening, March 28, the Amity Harbor High School senior ball—its theme this year was "Daffodil Daze"—went forward in the high school auditorium. An Anacortes swing band, Men About Town, played upbeat dance tunes exclusively; during an interlude the captain of the baseball team stood in front of the microphone on the bandstand and cheerfully handed out honorary letters to the seven team members departing Monday morning. "We don't have much chance without you," he said. "Right now we don't even have enough guys to field a team. But any wins we do get, they're for you guys who are leaving."

Evelyn Nearing, the animal lover—she was a widow who lived without a flush toilet or electricity in a cedar cabin on Yearsley Point—took goats, pigs, dogs, and cats from a half-dozen Japanese families. The Odas leased their grocery to the Charles MacPhersons and sold Charles their car and two pickup trucks. Arthur Chambers made arrangements with Nelson Obada to act as a special correspondent for his newspaper and to send reports to San Piedro. Arthur ran four articles on the imminent evacuation in his March 26 edition: "Island Japanese Accept Army Mandate to Move," "Japanese Ladies Praised for Last-Minute PTA Work," "Evacuation Order Hits Prep Baseball Nine," and a "Plain Talk" column called "Not Enough Time," which roundly condemned the relocation authority for its "pointless and merciless speed in exiling our island's Japanese-Americans. . . ."

Copyright © 1994 by David Guterson.

An Army truck took Fujiko and her five daughters to the Amity Harbor ferry dock at seven o'clock on Monday morning, where a soldier gave them tags for their suitcases and coats. They waited among their bags in the cold while their *hakujin* neighbors stood staring at them where they were gathered on the dock between the soldiers. Fujiko saw Ilse Severensen there, leaning against the railing with her hands clasped in front of her; she waved at the Imadas as they passed by. Ilse, a Seattle transplant, had for ten years purchased strawberries from Fujiko and spoke to her as if she were a peasant whose role in life was to make island life pleasantly exotic for Ilse's friends who visited from the city. Her kindness had always been condescending, and she had always paid a bit extra for her berries with the air of doling out charity. And so, on this morning, Fujiko could not meet her eyes or acknowledge her despite the fact that Ilse Severensen had waved and called out her name in a friendly way—Fujiko studied the ground instead; she kept her eyes cast down.

At nine o'clock they were marched on board the *Kehloken,* with the white people gaping at them from the hill above, and Gordon Tanaka's daughter—she was eight years old—fell on the dock and began to cry. Soon other people were crying, too, and from the hill came the voice of Antonio Dangaran, a Filipino man who had married Eleanor Kitano just two months before. "Eleanor!" he shouted, and when she looked up he let go a bouquet of red roses, which sailed gently toward the water in the wind and landed in the waves below the dock pilings.

They were taken from Anacortes on a train to a transit camp—the horse stables at the Puyallup fairgrounds. They lived in the horse stalls and slept on canvas army cots; at nine P.M. they were confined to their stalls; at ten P.M. they were made to turn out their lights, one bare bulb for each family. The cold in the stalls worked into their bones, and when it rained that night they moved their cots because of the leaks in the roof. The next morning, at six A.M., they slogged through mud to the transit camp mess hall and ate canned figs and white bread from pie tins and drank coffee out of tin cups. Through all of it Fujiko maintained her dignity, though she'd felt herself beginning to crack while relieving herself in front of other women.

After three days they boarded another train and began a languid crawl toward California. At night the MPs [military police] who roamed from car to car came through telling them to pull down their window shades, and they passed the dark hours twisting in their seats and exerting themselves not to complain. The train stopped and started and jolted them toward wakefulness, and there was a constant line at the door to the toilet. Fujiko did her best not to give in to her discomfort by speaking of it to her daughters. She did not want them to know that she was suffering inwardly and needed to lie down comfortably somewhere and sleep for a long time. For when she slept at all it was with her hearing tuned to the bluebottle flies always pestering her and to the crying of the Takami baby, who was three weeks old and had a fever. The wailing of this baby ate at her, and she rode with her fingers stuffed inside her ears, but this did not seem to change things. Her sympathy for the baby and for all of the Takamis began to slip as sleep evaded her, and she secretly began to wish for the baby's death if such a thing could mean silence. And at the same time she hated herself for thinking this and fought against it while her anger grew at the fact that the baby could not just be flung from the window so that the rest of them might have some peace. Then, long past the point when she had told herself that she could not endure another moment, the baby would stop its tortured shrieking, Fujiko would calm herself and close her eyes, retreat with enormous relief toward sleep, and then the Takami baby would once again wail and shriek inconsolably.

The train stopped at a place called Mojave in the middle of an interminable, still desert. They were herded onto buses at eight-thirty in the morning, and the buses took them north over dusty roads for four hours to a place called Manzanar. Fujiko had imagined, shutting her eyes, that the sandstorm battering the bus was the rain of home. She'd dozed and awakened in time to see the barbed wire and the rows of dark barracks blurred by blowing dust. It was twelve-thirty, by her watch; they were just in time

At nine o'clock they were marched on board the **Kehloken,** *with the white people gaping at them.*

to stand in line for lunch. They ate standing up, from army mess kits, with their backs turned against the wind. Peanut butter, white bread, canned figs, and string beans; she could taste the dust in all of it.

They were given typhoid shots that first afternoon; they stood in line for them. They waited in the dust beside their luggage and then stood in line for dinner. In the evening the Imadas were assigned to Block 11, Barrack 4, and given a sixteen-by-twenty-foot room furnished with a bare lightbulb, a small Coleman oil heater, six CCC camp cots, six straw mattresses, and a dozen army blankets. Fujiko sat on the edge of a cot with cramps from the camp food and the typhoid shot gathering to a knot in her stomach. She sat with her coat on, holding herself, while her daughters beat flat the straw in the mattresses and lit the oil heater. Even with the heater she shivered beneath her blankets, still fully dressed in her clothes. By midnight she couldn't wait any longer and, with three of her daughters who were feeling distressed too, stumbled out into the darkness of the desert in the direction of the block latrine. There was, astonishingly, a long line at midnight, fifty or more women and girls in heavy coats with their backs braced against the wind. A woman up the line vomited heavily, and the smell was of the canned figs they'd all eaten. The woman apologized profusely in Japanese, and then another in the line vomited, and they were all silent again.

That night dust and yellow sand blew through the knotholes in the walls and floor. By morning their blankets were covered with it. Fujiko's pillow lay white where her head had been, but around it a layer of fine yellow grains had gathered. She felt it against her face and in her hair and on the inside of her mouth, too. It had been a cold night, and in the adjacent room a baby screamed behind a quarter-inch wall of pine board.

On their second day at Manzanar they were given a mop, a broom, and a bucket. The leader of their block—a man from Los Angeles dressed in a dusty overcoat who claimed to have been an attorney in his former life but who now stood unshaven with one shoe untied and with his wire-rimmed glasses skewed on his face—showed them the outdoor water tap. Fujiko and her daughters cleaned out the dust and did laundry in a gallon-size soup tin. While they were cleaning more dust and sand blew in to settle on the newly mopped pine boards. Hatsue went out into the desert wind and returned with a few scraps of tar paper she'd found blown up against a roll of barbed wire along a firebreak. They stuffed this around the doorjamb and fixed it over the knotholes with thumbtacks borrowed from the Fujitas.

There was no sense in talking to anyone about things. Everyone was in the same position. Everyone wandered like ghosts beneath the guard towers with the mountains looming on either side of them. The bitter wind came down off the mountains and through the barbed wire and hurled the desert sand in their faces. The camp was only half-finished; there were not enough barracks to go around. Some people, on arriving, had to build their own in order to have a place to sleep. There were crowds everywhere, thousands of people in a square mile of desert scoured to dust by army bulldozers, and there was nowhere for a person to find solitude.

Copyright © 1994 by David Guterson.

Research Options

1. Use an encyclopedia, a history book, the Internet, or another source to research the internment of Japanese Americans during World War II. Then prepare a brief oral report for the class.
2. Fujiko and her daughters are sent to Manzanar in California. Find out where other Japanese-American internment camps were located in the United States. Then create a map labeling each site with the name of the camp that was situated there.

CHAPTER

17

Section 1

AMERICAN LIVES Oveta Culp Hobby
Skilled Administrator

"Mrs. Hobby has proved that a competent, efficient woman who works longer days than the sun does not need to look like the popular idea of a competent, efficient woman."—quoted in the Washington Times Herald (1942)

Oveta Culp Hobby's abilities helped her establish the place of women in the military and the government. During the first months of World War II, when the government decided to create an organization for women within the U.S. Army, she was picked as its director. Eleven years later, she was named head of the new Department of Health, Education, and Welfare.

Born the daughter of a Texas lawyer in 1905, Oveta Culp developed an interest in the law. After attending college, she took classes at the University of Texas Law School. At age 20, she was named parliamentarian for the Texas state legislature. Later she wrote a book on correct parliamentary procedure that became a standard text. In 1931, she married William Hobby, the publisher of the *Houston Post,* and began working for the paper. She introduced features that appealed to women readers. As her husband became involved in other businesses, she began to run the paper.

It was in government work, though, that Hobby made her most important contributions. In 1941 she joined the War Department as head of the Office of Public Relations. There she met General George C. Marshall, the army's chief of staff. The next year, Congress created the Women's Auxiliary Army Corps (WAAC). The goal was to train women to perform office work and other vital duties, freeing male soldiers for combat. Marshall tapped Hobby as the first head of the WAACs. In 1943, the unit's name was changed to the Women's Army Corps (WAC), and Hobby was promoted from major to colonel.

The WACs met some hostility both within and outside the military. Not everyone believed that women should serve in the armed forces. Hobby overcame the opposition, however, and built a strong organization. She dismissed reporters' questions about uniforms and other trivial matters. "This is a serious job for serious women," she said. By war's end, 100,000 women served in the unit. They handled a range of duties from office work to communications and supply. Some WACs even

joined the Manhattan Project, the secret effort to develop an atomic weapon. For her service, Hobby was given the Distinguished Service Medal, only the seventh woman so honored.

After resigning in 1945, Hobby returned to the Post and pursued business and charitable interests. She also remained active in politics, working in the successful campaign of Dwight Eisenhower for president in 1952.

Once in office, Eisenhower named Hobby to head the Federal Security Administration. That agency oversaw federal programs in education and social security. In 1953, the FSA was changed to the Department of Health, Education, and Welfare (HEW) and given Cabinet status. Hobby became the first secretary of HEW—only the second woman ever to hold a Cabinet post. In education, she worked to overcome a growing shortage of teachers and classrooms and to move toward the desegregation of schools.

In health administration, the department's main activity involved administering the distribution of polio vaccine. Polio was a serious infectious disease that caused paralysis and sometimes death in the most extreme cases. Parents feared for their children. In 1954, a new vaccine against polio was found to be successful. The federal government led a program to vaccinate millions of people–children first.

Hobby retired from HEW and public life in 1955. She returned to Houston and became president and editor of the *Post* and pursued broadcasting businesses. She also remained active in charity work, dying in 1995 at age 90.

Questions

1. Why did Hobby have to defend the WAC as a place for "serious women"?
2. How does the attitude toward the Women's Army Corps contrast with the view of women in the army today?
3. How does the article support the assertion that Oveta Culp Hobby was a skilled administrator?

CHAPTER

17

Section 2

AMERICAN LIVES George S. Patton
Bold Leader, Undisciplined Follower

"This man would be invaluable in time of war, but is a disturbing element in time of peace."—General W. R. Smith on George S. Patton (1927)

George S. Patton was ideally suited to command an army. He was a bold strategist and a good administrator who knew how to motivate his troops. However, his boldness also led him to words and actions that caused political difficulties.

Patton (1885–1945) was born to a family with an army tradition; his grandfather had been killed in a Civil War battle. After graduating from West Point in 1909, Patton immediately entered the army. During World War I, he watched the British use the first tanks in combat. He quickly saw the advantages of the new weapon and helped organize an American tank force. When the United States entered the war, he led his unit into combat and fought well. By staying in the field despite a serious wound, he earned two medals.

Between the two world wars, Patton held various posts while pursuing his hobbies—riding and hunting, boating, and military history. In 1940, as war raged in Europe, Patton was given command of part of an armored division at a base in Georgia, which included tanks in its equipment. He got an ill-trained, ill-equipped unit into shape.

After the United States entered World War II, Patton played a vital role—and repeatedly got in trouble. He was given command of one of the Allied armies invading North Africa. There they faced troops of a fascist French government that—after the fall of France—had joined itself with Nazi Germany. Patton's armored force moved quickly through their defenses. Afterward, though, Patton's reputation was hurt by charges that he had entertained people with pro-Nazi sentiments at his North African villa. Patton was saved when General Dwight Eisenhower removed him and put him in charge of another combat unit.

The American soldiers had just lost their first North African battle with the Germans. British commanders complained that the U.S. II Armored Corps was unfit to fight. Patton took charge, removing officers who were not aggressive and using discipline and colorful speeches to raise morale. His corps won a number of battles, helping force the Germans to leave North Africa.

Next Patton was given command of the American troops invading Sicily. He landed and moved his force quickly around the western edge of the island—against orders. The American troops pushed the Germans off Sicily, gaining cheers from the Italians and headlines for Patton. His popularity fell almost as quickly, though. News reports revealed that he had slapped two soldiers who were suffering combat fatigue, believing that they were faking their condition. Many called for Patton's dismissal. Eisenhower did remove him from command, but refused to send him back to America. His new job now was to prepare to follow up the invasion of France planned for 1944.

Patton's Third Army reached France shortly after the Normandy invasion. It quickly drove the Germans out of northern France. Effectively using air support, ground troops, and tanks, Patton pushed across the north of France to the German border. Lack of supplies stalled the drive, and combat settled into a stalemate. In December of 1944, the Germans launched their last offensive, pushing deeply into the Allies' lines north of Patton. With remarkable speed, he changed his army's direction to counterattack and force a withdrawal. Experts call it one of the most brilliant moves in the war.

When the war in Europe ended, Patton got in trouble again. He greatly feared the power of the Soviet Union and proposed that U.S. forces join with the remaining German troops to drive the Russian army in Germany back to its national boundaries. After he made these statements publicly, he was assigned to a desk job. He died later that year in a car accident in Germany.

Questions

1. What details show Patton's skill as a commander?
2. Why do you think Eisenhower never removed Patton from command despite the problems he caused?
3. Why did Patton's comments on the Soviet Union cause difficulty?

CHAPTER
18
Section 1

GUIDED READING *Origins of the Cold War*

A. As you read this section, complete the cause-and-effect diagram with the specific
U.S. actions made in response to the Soviet actions listed. Use the following terms
and names in filling out the diagram:

containment   **Truman Doctrine**   **Berlin airlift**   **NATO**

Cause: Soviet Action

Soviet leader Joseph Stalin
refused free elections in Eastern
Europe and set up satellite
nations.

Effect: U.S. Action

1.

Effect: U.S. Action

2.

Cause: Soviet Action

Soviets blockaded Berlin for
almost a year.

Effect: U.S. Action

3.

Effect: U.S. Action

4.

B. On the back of this paper, explain the significance of each of the following terms:

Cold War   **Marshall Plan**

Name _____ Date _____

GUIDED READING *The Cold War Heats Up*

A. As you read this section, fill out the chart below by writing answers to the questions in the appropriate boxes.

	Civil War in China	Civil War in Korea
1. Which side did the United States support, and why?		
2. What did the United States do to affect the outcome of the war?		
3. What was the outcome of the war?		
4. How did the American public react to that outcome, and why?		

B. On the back of this paper, explain the significance of each of the following terms and names:

Mao Zedong   Chiang Kai-shek   Taiwan (Formosa)   38th parallel

Name _____ Date _____

A. As you read this section, fill out the charts below by writing answers to the
questions in the appropriate boxes.

	a. What were they accused of ?	b. How were they affected by the accusations?	c. Do the accusations seem to have been fair? Explain.
1. The Hollywood Ten			
2. Alger Hiss			
3. Ethel and Julius Rosenberg			

McCarthyism		
4. What seems to have motivated it?	5. Why did it succeed at first?	6. Why did it fall out of favor?

B. On the back of this paper, explain the significance of each of the following terms
and names:

    HUAC   **blacklist**   **Senator Joseph McCarthy**

CHAPTER 18

Section 4

GUIDED READING *Two Nations Live on the Edge*

A. As you read this section, write your answers to the question in the appropriate boxes.

	How did the United States react, and why?
1. The Soviet Union exploded its first atomic bomb in 1949.	
2. In 1951, the Iranian prime minister placed the oil industry in Iran under the Iranian government's control.	
3. The Guatemalan head of government gave American-owned land in Guatemala to peasants.	
4. In 1956, Britain, France, and Israel invaded Egypt and occupied the Suez Canal.	
5. Soviet tanks invaded Hungary and fired on protesters in 1956.	
6. In 1957, the Soviet Union launched Sputnik.	
7. In 1960, the Soviet Union brought down an American U-2 piloted by Francis Gary Powers.	

B. On the back of this paper, explain the significance of each of the following terms and names:

| H-bomb | brinkmanship | Nikita Khrushchev | Warsaw Pact |
| CIA | Eisenhower Doctrine | Dwight D. Eisenhower | John Foster Dulles |

A. Matching Match the description in the second column with person or term in the first column. Write the appropriate letter next to the word.

_____ 1. U-2 incident   a. coalition of Eastern European nations

_____ 2. United Nations   b. dividing line between North and South Korea

_____ 3. Marshall Plan   c. U.S. effort to rebuild nations of Europe

_____ 4. John Foster Dulles   d. world peacekeeping body

_____ 5. Alger Hiss   e. policy of stopping the spread of communism

_____ 6. 38th parallel   f. downing of U.S. spy plane over Soviet Union

_____ 7. containment   g. alleged spy for the Soviet Union

_____ 8. Warsaw Pact   h. staunchly anti-Communist Secretary of State

B. Multiple Choice Circle the letter before the term or name that best completes the sentence.

1. The leader of the Soviet Union who succeeded Joseph Stalin was (a) Nikita Khrushchev (b) Gamal Abdel-Nasser (c) Jawaharlal Nehru.

2. In China's civil war, the Communist faction was led by (a) Chiang Kai-shek (b) Kim Il Sung (c) Mao Zedong.

3. The pledge by the United States to defend Middle East countries from Communist takeovers was known as the (a) Truman Doctrine (b) Eisenhower Doctrine (c) Warsaw Pact.

4. The conflict between the United States and the Soviet Union in which neither side directly confronted the other on the battlefield was known as (a) brinkmanship (b) containment (c) the Cold War.

5. Francis Gary Powers, who became a prominent figure of the Cold War as a result of the U-2 incident, was a (a) pilot (b) congressman (c) writer.

C. Writing Write a paragraph about the anti-Communist hysteria that gripped the United States during World War II using the following terms.

HUAC   **Hollywood Ten**   **blacklist**   **McCarthyism**

CHAPTER **18**

Section 1

SKILLBUILDER PRACTICE *Analyzing Motives*

How did the Cold War develop so soon after the success of the Allied victory in World War II? When you analyze the motives of the United States and the Soviet Union at the end of the war, look at the experiences, emotions, and needs that compelled each nation to act in a certain way. Read the following passage, and then complete the chart below. (See Skillbuilder Handbook, p. R6.)

U.S. and Soviet War Experiences The Soviet Union suffered more casualties in World War II than all the other Allies combined. The Soviet Red Army lost approximately 7.5 million soldiers, more than twice Germany's loss of about 3.5 million. Moreover, there were about 19 million Soviet civilians killed during the war and another 25 million refugees left homeless. Much of Russia, Poland, and the Ukraine lay in ruins, having been overrun and scorched several times during the fighting.

Although 405,000 U.S. soldiers died in the war, there were no civilian casualties, and the continental United States was never invaded or bombed. The industrial production necessitated by the war helped the country out of the Depression and revitalized its capitalist economy. By 1945, almost half of all the goods and services produced in the world came from the United States.

U.S. and Soviet Goals It was clear even before the end of the war that the United States and the Soviet Union had different goals for Europe.

The United States wanted to rebuild Europe, especially Germany, so that the burden of feeding so many refugees would not fall on American tax-

payers. It was also in U.S. interests to have economically strong European countries that were able to buy U.S. products. The Soviet Union, on the other hand, wanted to rebuild itself. Stalin thought Germany should pay $20 million in machinery and raw material as reparations for the wrongs the Soviets had suffered during the war.

After the Soviet experience in the war, Stalin feared invasion from the West. Gaining military and political control of Eastern Europe was his way of creating a buffer from further attack. Since the Red Army occupied the countries it liberated from the Germans, Stalin quickly set up or supported similar Communist governments. According to Stalin, "In this war, each side imposes its system as far as its armies can reach. It cannot be otherwise."

For its part, the United States feared totalitarian regimes that imposed their own systems on otherwise free and independent nations. Stalin in his desire for absolute control, Truman argued, was every bit as ruthless and dangerous as Hitler. Truman's efforts to contain communism was a diplomatic compromise between going to war again and stopping the Soviets from gaining any more power in the world than they already had.

	Experiences During War	Emotions After War	Needs After War
SOVIET UNION			
UNITED STATES			

Reading Comprehension

Choose the best answer for each item. Write the letter of your answer in the blank.

_____ 1. The world peacekeeping body formed after World War II was called the
     a. League of Nations.
     b. United Nations.
     c. North Atlantic Treaty Organization.
     d. Warsaw Pact.

_____ 2. The now-famous "iron curtain" speech was given by
     a. Harry S. Truman.
     b. Douglas MacArthur.
     c. Winston Churchill.
     d. George Marshall.

_____ 3. All of the following were considered satellite nations of the Soviet Union except
     a. Greece.
     b. Poland.
     c. Hungary.
     d. Czechoslovakia.

_____ 4. The amount of aid provided to European countries from the Marshall Plan totaled about
     a. $6 billion.
     b. $10 billion.
     c. $13 billion.
     d. $20 billion.

_____ 5. One of the key characteristics of communism was
     a. no opposing parties.
     b. a market-based economy.
     c. free and open elections.
     d. a weak central government.

_____ 6. All of the following were members of NATO except
     a. China.
     b. France.
     c. the Netherlands.
     d. the United States.

Sequencing

A. Complete the time line below by describing the key events of the Korean War.

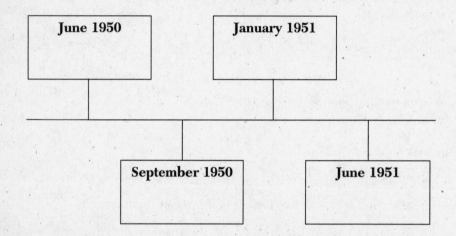

June 1950		January 1951
September 1950		June 1951

Finding Main Ideas

B. Answer the following questions in the space provided.

1. What was the reaction in America to the Communist takeover of China?

_____

_____

2. Why did President Truman fire General MacArthur?

_____

_____

3. How did the stalemate in Korea impact the U.S. political scene?

_____

_____

Summarizing

A. Complete the chart below by describing how each term listed below demonstrated the nation's anti-Communist hysteria.

Hollywood Ten	
The Rosenberg Trial	
McCarthyism	

Evaluating

B. *T* in the blank if the statement is true. If the statement is false, write *F* in the blank and then write the corrected statement on the line below.

_____ 1. The McCarran Internal Security Act made it unlawful to plan any action that might lead to the establishment of a dictatorship in the United States.

_____

_____ 2. Joseph McCarthy first rose to popularity by pursuing charges against alleged state department spy Alger Hiss.

_____

_____ 3. Joseph McCarthy's downfall came after he made Communist-related accusations against the White House.

_____

RETEACHING ACTIVITY *Two Nations Live on the Edge*

Matching

A. Match the description in the second column with term or name in the first column. Write the appropriate letter next to the word.

_____ 1. Central Intelligence Agency   a. prompted conflict by seizing Suez Canal

_____ 2. Guatemala   b. world's first artificial satellite

_____ 3. Shah of Iran   c. engaged in covert operations abroad

_____ 4. *Sputnik*   d. alliance of Eastern European countries

_____ 5. Warsaw Pact   e. Middle East ally of the United States

_____ 6. Gamel Abdel Nassar   f. site of covert CIA activities

Completion

B. Complete each sentence with the appropriate term or name.

Eisenhower Doctrine	brinkmanship
Spain	Hungary
space race	Truman Doctrine
Israel	Czechoslovakia

1. In 1956, the Soviets brutally put down a pro-democracy rebellion in _____.

2. The _____ stated that the United States would defend the Middle East against the spread of communism.

3. The U.S.-Soviet competition for supremacy of the earth's orbit was know as the _____.

4. The three nations that confronted Egypt over its seizure of the Suez Canal were France, Great Britain, and _____.

5. The policy of going to the edge of all-out war is known as _____.

CHAPTER
18
Section 1

GEOGRAPHY APPLICATION: REGION *The Marshall Plan*

Directions: Read the paragraphs below and study the graph carefully. Then answer the questions that follow.

When World War II ended and the countries of Europe needed emergency relief and economic aid, the United States, Canada, and other nations contributed to the effort. Despite their efforts, necessities were still in short supply. In some countries, food was even scarcer than it had been during the war. To determine the full extent of the problem, President Truman sent former President Herbert Hoover on a fact-finding mission to 22 European nations. On his return, Hoover reported the stark reality to Truman. People were starving in Europe, and stopgap aid would not solve the problem. A long-term plan was needed.

During a Harvard College commencement address in June 1947, Secretary of State George C. Marshall offered the aid of the United States to all European nations in need. He asked the nations of Europe to agree on a plan of recovery and to tell the United States what aid was needed. In return for the aid of the United States, Marshall proposed that European nations would have to agree to cooperate and remove trade barriers. Although invited to participate, the Soviet Union refused Marshall's offer. In addition, the Soviets prevented their satellite nations in Eastern Europe from applying for aid.

In all, 16 Western European countries applied for assistance under what was known as the European Recovery Program, or the Marshall Plan. Congress heatedly debated the plan for ten months. The loudest and most insistent criticism concerned the estimated cost—about $12.5 billion. For a time, it looked as if Congress would reject the plan. However, in February 1948, a Soviet-backed uprising put Communists in control of Czechoslovakia. Alarmed by this Soviet aggression, Congress promptly approved the Marshall Plan by large majorities in both houses.

The Marshall Plan proved to be a great success, both politically and economically. The spread of communism was halted, and Western European economies quickly revived. Within three years, the production of goods in Western Europe surpassed prewar levels. The Marshall Plan also proved beneficial to the American economy, for an economically revitalized Western Europe provided a ready market for American goods and services.

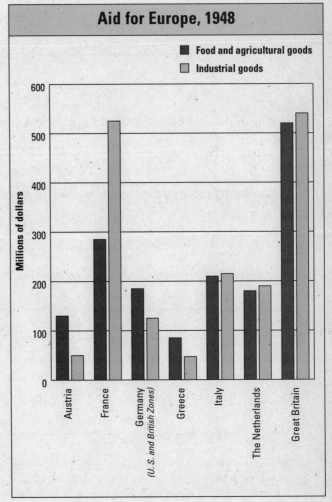

Aid for Europe, 1948

■ Food and agricultural goods
□ Industrial goods

Millions of dollars

(Bar chart with y-axis from 0 to 600, showing aid by country: Austria, France, Germany (U.S. and British Zones), Greece, Italy, The Netherlands, Great Britain)

Interpreting Text and Graphics

1. What commodity was particularly scarce in Europe after the war? _____

2. Which two countries on the graph received the most total aid in 1948, the first
   year of the Marshall Plan? _____

   Why do you suppose this was true? _____

   _____

   _____

   _____

3. Why do you think the Soviet Union opposed the Marshall Plan? _____

   _____

   _____

   _____

4. How many dollars worth of food and agricultural aid did Italy receive in 1948?

   _____

5. Which country received the most in total aid in 1948? _____

   What was the total dollar amount, approximately? _____

6. What event finally moved Congress to approve the Marshall Plan? _____

   _____

   _____

7. In your own words, explain the following statement: "The Marshall Plan saved
   Western Europe from being absorbed into the Soviet Bloc." _____

   _____

   _____

   _____

   _____

CHAPTER

18

Section 1

PRIMARY SOURCE *from* Harry S. Truman's
Letter to His Daughter

In this excerpt, Truman tells of first becoming president and of his meeting with Churchill and Stalin at the Potsdam Conference near Berlin. As you read, think about the challenges Truman faced at the beginning of his presidency.

As you know I was Vice-President from Jan. 20 to April 12, 1945. I was at Cabinet meetings and saw Roosevelt once or twice in those months. But he never did talk to me confidentially about the war, or about foreign affairs or what he had in mind for the peace after the war. . . .

Well the catastrophe we all dreaded came on April 12 at 4:35 P.M. At 7:09 I was the President and my first decision was to go ahead with the San Francisco Conference to set up the U.N.

Then I had to start in reading memorandums, briefs, and volumes of correspondence on the World situation. Too bad I hadn't been on the Foreign Affairs Committee or that F.D.R. hadn't informed me on the situation. . . . Then Germany folded up. You remember that celebration that took place on May 8, 1945—my 61st birthday.

Then came Potsdam. . . . Stalin was a day late, Churchill was on hand when I arrived, I found the Poles in eastern Germany without authority and Russia in possession of East Prussia, Latvia, Estonia and Lithuania, as well as Rumania and Bulgaria. Churchill had urged me to send our troops to the eastern border of Germany and keep them there.

We were about 150 miles east of the border of the occupation zone line agreed to at Yalta. I felt that agreements made in the war to keep Russia fighting should be kept and I kept them to the letter. Perhaps they should not have been adhered to so quickly. . . . Perhaps if we had been slower moving back we could have forced the Russians, Poles, Bulgars, Yugos etc. to behave. But all of us wanted Russia in the Japanese War. Had we known what the Atomic Bomb would do we'd have never have wanted the Bear [symbol of Russia] in the picture. You must remember no tests had been made until several days after I arrived in Berlin [for the Potsdam Conference].

Adm. Leahy told me that he was an explosives expert and Roosevelt had just thrown $2,600,000,000 away for nothing. He was wrong. But his guess was as good as any. [Senator Jim] Byrnes thought it [the A-bomb] might work but he wasn't sure. He thought if it did we would win the Japanese War without much more losses but we still needed the Russians. That was one of my prime objects in going to Berlin—to get the Russians into the Jap War. Well, many agreements were made at Potsdam, the Foreign Minister's Conference was set up, I suggested that the Danube, the Rhine, . . . the Black Sea Straits all be made free waterways and that no trade barriers be set up in Europe. The last suggestion got nowhere. Had it been adopted all Europe's and the World's troubles would have been half over.

We entered into agreements for the Government of Germany—not one of which has Russia kept. We made agreements on China, Korea and other places none of which has Russia kept. So that now we are faced with exactly the same situation with which Britain + France were faced in 1938/39 with Hitler. A totalitarian state is no different whether you call it Nazi, Fascist, Communist or Franco's Spain.

Things look black. We've offered control and disarmament through the U.N., giving up our one most powerful weapon for the world to control. The Soviets won't agree. They're upsetting things in Korea, in China, in Persia (Iran) and in the Near East.

A decision will have to be made. I am going to make it. I am sorry to have bored you with this. But you've studied foreign affairs to some extent and I just wanted you to know your dad as President asked for no territory, no reparations, no slave laborers—only Peace in the World.

from Margaret Truman, ed., *Letters from Father: The Truman Family's Personal Correspondence* (New York: Arbor House, 1981), 103–108.

Discussion Questions

1. According to his letter, what challenges did Truman face when he became president?
2. What does Truman's letter reveal about his attitude toward the Soviet Union?
3. How well do you think Truman handled foreign affairs right after he became president? What could he have done differently?

CHAPTER
18

Section 2

PRIMARY SOURCE *from* Douglas MacArthur's Farewell Address to Congress

President Truman's dismissal of General MacArthur as Commander of the UN forces in Korea sparked debate in Congress over Truman's strategy of fighting a limited war in Korea. MacArthur was asked to address a Joint Session of Congress as part of the congressional investigation into this issue. What follows is an excerpt of MacArthur's speech in which he defends his position. As you read his speech, pay attention to the reasons he gives for expanding the war and decide whether you agree with him.

Mr. President, Mr. Speaker, and distinguished members of the Congress:

I stand on this rostrum with a sense of deep humility and great pride—humility in the wake of those great American architects of our history who have stood here before me, pride in the reflection that this forum of legislative debate represents human liberty in the purest form yet devised. Here are centered the hopes, and aspirations, and faith of the entire human race.

I do not stand here as advocate for any partisan cause, for the issues are fundamental and reach quite beyond the realm of partisan consideration. They must be resolved on the highest plane of national interest if our course is to prove sound and our future protected. I trust, therefore, that you will do me the justice of receiving that which I have to say as solely expressing the considered viewpoint of a fellow American. I address you with neither rancor nor bitterness in the fading twilight of life with but one purpose in mind—to serve my country. . . .

I now turn to the Korean conflict. While I was not consulted prior to the President's decision to intervene in support of the Republic of Korea, that decision from a military standpoint proved a sound one as we hurled back the invaders and decimated his forces. Our victory was complete and our objectives within reach when Red China intervened with numerically superior ground forces. This created a new war and an entirely new situation—a situation not contemplated when our forces were committed against the North Korean invaders— a situation which called for new decisions in the diplomatic sphere to permit the realistic adjustment of military strategy. Such decisions have not been forthcoming.

While no man in his right mind would advocate sending our ground forces into continental China, and such was never given a thought, the new situation did urgently demand a drastic revision of strategic planning if our political aim was to defeat this new enemy as we had defeated the old.

Apart from the military need as I saw it to neutralize the sanctuary protection given the enemy north of the Yalu, I felt that military necessity in the conduct of the war made mandatory:

1. The intensification of our economic blockade against China.

2. The imposition of a naval blockade against the China coast.

3. Removal of restrictions on air reconnaissance of China's coast areas and of Manchuria.

4. Removal of restriction on the forces of the Republic of China on Formosa [Taiwan] with logistical support to contribute to their effective operations against the common enemy.

For entertaining these views, all professionally designed to support our forces committed to Korea and bring hostilities to an end with the least possible delay and at a saving of countless American and Allied lives, I have been severely criticized in lay circles, principally abroad, despite my understanding that from a military standpoint the above views have been fully shared in the past by practically every military leader concerned with the Korean campaign, including our own Joint Chiefs of Staff.

I called for reinforcements, but was informed that reinforcements were not available. I made clear that if not permitted to destroy the buildup bases north of the Yalu; if not permitted to utilize the friendly Chinese force of some 600,000 men on Formosa [Taiwan]; if not permitted to blockade the China coast to prevent the Chinese Reds from getting succor from without; and if there were to be no hope of major reinforcements, the position of the command from the military standpoint forbade victory. We could hold in Korea by constant maneuver and at an approximate area where our supply line advantages were in balance with the supply line disadvantages of the enemy, but we could hope at best for only an indecisive campaign, with its terrible and constant attrition upon our forces if the enemy utilized his full military potential.

I have constantly called for the new political decisions essential to a solution. Efforts have been made to distort my position. It has been said, in effect, that I am a warmonger. Nothing can be further from the truth. I know war as few other men now living know it, and nothing to me is more revolting. I have long advocated its complete abolition as its very destructiveness on both friend and foe has rendered it useless as a means of settling international disputes. . . .

But once war if forced upon us, there is no other alternative than to apply every available means to bring it to a swift end. War's very object is victory—not prolonged indecision. In war, indeed, there can be no substitute for victory.

There are some who for varying reasons would appease Red China. They are blind to history's clear lesson; for history teaches with unmistakable emphasis that appeasement but begets new and bloodier war. It points to no single instance where the end has justified that means—where appeasement has led to more than a sham peace. Like blackmail, it lays the basis for new and successively greater demands, until, as in blackmail, violence becomes the only other alternative.

Why, my soldiers asked of me, surrender military advantages to an enemy in the field? I could not answer. Some may say to avoid spread of the conflict into an all-out war with China; others, to avoid Soviet intervention. Neither explanation seems valid. For China is already engaging with the maximum power it can commit and the Soviet will not necessarily mesh its actions with our moves. Like a cobra, any new enemy will more likely strike whenever it feels that the relativity in military or other potential is in its favor on a worldwide basis.

The tragedy of Korea is further heightened by the fact that as military action is confined to its territorial limits, it condemns that nation, which it is our purpose to save, to suffer the devastating impact of full naval and air bombardment, while the enemy's sanctuaries are fully protected from such attack and devastation. Of the nations of the world, Korea alone, up to now, is the sole one which has risked its all against communism. The magnificence of the courage and fortitude of the Korean people defies description. They have chosen to risk death rather than slavery. Their last words to me were, "Don't scuttle the Pacific."

I have just left your fighting sons in Korea. They have met all tests there and I can report to you without reservation they are splendid in every way. It was my constant effort to preserve them and end this savage conflict honorably and with the least loss of time and a minimum sacrifice of life. Its growing bloodshed has caused me the deepest anguish and anxiety. Those gallant men will remain often in my thoughts in my prayers always.

I am closing my fifty-two years of military service. When I joined the Army, even before the turn of the century, it was the fulfillment of all my boyish hopes and dreams. The world has turned over many times since I took the oath on the plain at West Point, and the hopes and dreams have long since vanished. But I still remember the refrain of one of the most popular barrack ballads of that day which proclaimed most proudly that—

Old soldiers never die;
they just fade away.

And like the old soldier of that ballad, I now close my military career and just fade away—an old soldier who tried to do his duty as God gave him the light to see that duty.

Good-by.

from The 82nd Congress, 1st Session, *House Doc. No. 36*

Discussion Questions

1. What parts of this speech excerpt do you find the most persuasive? the least persuasive?
2. What do you think MacArthur's attitude in this speech is? To get a sense of his attitude, try reading parts of the speech aloud as you think he might have delivered it. Then, cite words and phrases from the speech as evidence to support your opinion.
3. After its investigation, Congress failed to agree on whether to continue Truman's policy of a limited war in Korea. If you had been a member of Congress at the time, how would you had voted? Cite evidence from your textbook, as well as from MacArthur's speech, to support your opinion.

CHAPTER 18

Section 4

PRIMARY SOURCE *from* Dwight D. Eisenhower's
Statement on the U-2 Incident

When Nikita Khrushchev announced that an American U-2 had been shot down over Soviet territory, U.S. officials at first denied that the U-2 was a spy plane. Then, President Dwight D. Eisenhower decided to tell the truth in a TV and radio broadcast. As you read this excerpt from his speech, keep in mind the reasons he gives for spying on the Soviets.

Our safety, and that of the free world, demand, of course, effective systems for gathering information about the military capabilities of other powerful nations, especially those that make a fetish of secrecy. This involves many techniques and methods. In these times of vast military machines and nuclear-tipped missiles, the ferreting out of this information is indispensable to free-world security. . . .

I take full responsibility for approving all the various programs undertaken by our government to secure and evaluate military intelligence.

It was in the prosecution of one of these intelligence programs that the widely publicized U-2 incident occurred.

Aerial photography has been one of many methods we have used to keep ourselves and the free world abreast of major Soviet military developments. The usefulness of this work has been well established through four years of effort. The Soviets were well aware of it. . . . Only last week, in his Paris press conference, Chairman Khrushchev confirmed that he knew of these flights when he visited the United States last September.

Incidentally, this raises the natural question—why all the furor concerning one particular flight? He did not, when in America last September, charge that these flights were any threat to Soviet safety. He did not then see any reason to refuse to confer with American representatives. This he did only about the flight that unfortunately failed, on May 1, far inside Russia.

Now, two questions have been raised about this particular flight: first, as to its timing, considering the imminence of the summit meeting; second, our initial statement when we learned the flight had failed.

As to the timing, the question was really whether to halt the program and thus forgo the gathering of important information that was essential and that was likely to be unavailable at a later date. The decision was that the program should not be halted. The plain truth is this: When a nation needs intelligence activity, there is no time when vigilance can be relaxed. Incidentally, from Pearl Harbor we learned that even negotiation itself can be used to conceal preparations for a surprise attack.

Next, as to our government's initial statement about the flight, this was issued to protect the pilot, his mission, and our intelligence processes, at a time when the true facts were still undetermined.

Our first information about the failure of this mission did not disclose whether the pilot was still alive, was trying to escape, was avoiding interrogation, or whether both plane and pilot had been destroyed. Protection of our intelligence system and the pilot, and concealment of the plane's mission, seemed imperative. . . .

I then made two facts clear to the public: first, our program of aerial reconnaissance had been undertaken with my approval; second, this government is compelled to keep abreast, by one means or another, of military activities of the Soviets, just as their government has for years engaged in espionage activities in our country and throughout the world.

from *Department of State Bulletin,* June 6, 1960, pp. 899–903

Discussion Questions

1. What reasons does Eisenhower give for gathering information about the Soviet military?
2. In your opinion, was the United States right to spy on the Soviets during the Cold War? Support your opinion with facts and reasons.

LITERATURE SELECTION *from* ***The Nuclear Age***
by Tim O'Brien

CHAPTER **18**

Section 4

The main character of this novel, 49-year-old William Cowling, grew up under the dark cloud of anxiety that loomed during the height of the Cold War. In this excerpt, Cowling recalls how he reacted to the threat of nuclear attack when he was a teenager in the 1950s. As you read, think about the steps Cowling takes to protect himself. Do you think his plan could help him survive a nuclear war?

When I was a kid, I converted my Ping-Pong table into a fallout shelter. Funny? Poignant? A nifty comment on the modern age? Well, let me tell you something. The year was 1958, and I was scared. Who knows how it started? Maybe it was all that CONELRAD stuff on the radio, tests of the Emergency Broadcast System, pictures of H-bombs in *Life* magazine, strontium 90 in the milk, the times in school when we'd crawl under our desks and cover our heads in practice for the real thing. Or maybe it was rooted deep inside me. In my own inherited fears, in the genes, in a coded conviction that the world wasn't safe for human life.

Really, who knows?

Whatever the sources, I was a frightened child. At night I'd toss around in bed for hours, battling the snagged sheets, and then when sleep finally came, sometimes close to dawn, my dreams would be clotted with sirens and melting ice caps and radioactive gleamings and ICBMs whining in the dark.

I was a witness. I saw it happen. In dreams, in imagination, I watched the world end. . . .

Even as a kid, maybe because I was a kid, I understood that there was nothing make-believe about doomsday. No hocus-pocus. No midnight fantasy. I knew better. It was real, like physics, like the laws of combustion and gravity. I could truly see it: a sleek nose cone, the wiring and dials and tangled circuitry. Real firepower, real danger. I was normal, yes, stable and levelheaded, but I was also willing to face the truth.

Anyway, I didn't have much choice. The nightmares had been squeezing my sleep for months, and finally, on a night in early May, a very quiet night, I woke up dizzy. My eyeballs ached. Things were so utterly silent I feared I'd gone deaf. Absolute silence. I sat up and wiped my face and waited for the world to rebalance itself. I'd been dreaming of

war—whole continents on fire, oceans boiling, cities in ash—and now, with that dreadful silence, it seemed that the universe had died in its sleep.

I was a child. There were few options.

I scrambled out of bed, put on my slippers, and ran for the basement. No real decision, I just did it.

Basement, I thought.

I went straight for the Ping-Pong table.

Shivering, wide awake, I began piling scraps of lumber and bricks and old rugs onto the table, making a thick roof, shingling it with a layer of charcoal briquettes to soak up the deadly radiation. I fashioned walls out of cardboard boxes filled with newspapers and two-by-fours and whatever basement junk I could find. I built a ventilation shaft out of cardboard tubing. I stocked the shelter with rations from the kitchen pantry, laid in a supply of bottled water, set up a dispensary of Band-Aids and iodine, designed my own little fallout mask.

When all this was finished, near dawn, I crawled under the table and lay there faceup, safe, arms folded across my chest.

I was a child. There were few options.

And, yes, I slept. No dreams.

My father found me down there. Still half asleep, I heard him calling out my name in a voice so distant, so muffled and hollow, that it might've come from another planet.

I didn't answer.

A door opened, lights clicked on. I watched my father's slippers glide across the concrete floor.

"William?" he said.

I sank deeper into my shelter.

"Hey, cowboy," my father said. "Out."

His voice had a stern, echoing sound. It made me coil up.

"Out," he repeated.

I could see the blue veins in his ankles. "Okay, in a minute," I told him. "I'm sort of busy right now."

My father stood still for a moment, then shuffled to the far end of the table. His slippers made a whish-whish noise. "Listen here," he said, "it's a swell little fort, a dandy, but you can't—"

"It's not a fort," I said.

"No?"

And so I explained it to him. How, in times like these, we needed certain safeguards. A line of defense against the man-made elements. A fallout shelter.

My father sneezed.

He cleared his throat and muttered something. Then, suddenly, in one deft motion, he bent down and grabbed me by the ankles and yanked me out from under the table.

Oddly, he was smiling.

"William," he murmured. "What's this?"

"What?"

"This. Right here."

Learning forward, still smiling, he jabbed a finger at my nose. At first I didn't understand.

"Oh, yeah," I said. "It's a fallout mask."

Actually, of course, it was just a paper bag filled with sawdust and charcoal briquettes. The bag had ventilation holes in it, and the whole contraption was attached to my face by strings and elastic bands. I grinned and started to show him how it worked, but my father raised his arm in a quick jerky movement, like a traffic cop, as if to warn me about something, then he squeezed my shoulder.

"Upstairs," he said. "On the double. Right now."

He seemed upset.

He pulled the mask off and marched me up the stairs, coming on strong with all that fatherly stuff about how I could've caught pneumonia, how he had enough to worry about without finding his kid asleep under a Ping-Pong table. All the while he kept glancing at me with those sharp blue eyes, half apprehensive and half amused, measuring.

When we got up to the kitchen, he showed my mother the mask. "Go ahead," he said, "guess what it is." But he didn't give her a chance. "A fallout mask. See there? Regulation fallout mask."

My mother smiled.

"Lovely," she said.

Then my father told her about the Ping-Pong table. He didn't openly mock me; he was subtle about it—a certain change of tone, raising his eyebrows when he thought I wasn't looking. But I was looking. And it made me wince. "The Ping-Pong table," he said slowly, "it's now a fallout shelter. Get it? A fallout shelter." He stretched the words out like rubber bands, letting them snap back hard: "Fallout shelter. Ping-Pong."

"It's sweet," my mother said, and her eyes did a funny rolling trick, then she laughed.

"Fallout," my father kept saying.

Again, they didn't mean to be cruel. But even after they'd scooted me in for a hot bath, I could hear them hooting it up, making jokes, finally tiptoeing down to the basement for a peek at my handiwork. I didn't see the humor in it.

Over breakfast, I tried to explain that radiation could actually kill you. Pure poison, I told them.

Or it could turn you into a mutant or a dwarf or something. "I mean, cripes," I said, "don't you guys even think about it, don't you worry?" I was confused. I couldn't understand those sly smiles. Didn't they read the newspapers? Hadn't they seen pictures of people who'd been exposed to radioactivity— hair burned off, bleeding tongues, teeth falling out, skin curled up like charred paper? Where was the joke in all that?

Somehow, though, I started feeling defensive, almost guilty, so finally I shut up and finished my pancakes and hustled off to school. God, I thought, am I crazy?

But that didn't end it.

All day long I kept thinking about the shelter, figuring ways to improve on it, drawing diagrams, calculating, imagining how I'd transform that plywood table into a real bastion against total war. In art class, I drew up elaborate renovation blueprints; in study hall, I devised a makeshift system for the decontamination of water supplies; during noon recess, while the rest of the kids screwed around, I began compiling a detailed list of items essential to human survival.

No question, it was nuke fever. But I wasn't wacko. In fact, I felt fully sane—tingling, in control.

In a way, I suppose, I was pushed on by the memory of that snug, dreamless sleep in my shelter. Cozy and walled in and secure. Like the feeling you

> *Over breakfast, I tried to explain that radiation could actually kill you. Pure poison, I told them.*

get in a tree house, or in a snow fort, or huddled around a fire at night. I'll even admit that my motives may have been anchored in some ancestral craving for refuge, the lion's instinct for the den, the impulse that first drove our species into caves. Safety, it's normal. The mole in his hole. The turtle in his shell. Look at history: the Alamo, castles on the Rhine, moated villages, turrets, frontier stockades, storm cellars, foxholes, barbed wire, an attic in Amsterdam, a cave along the Dead Sea. Besides, you can't ignore the realities. You can't use psychology to explain away the bomb.

> *No question, it was nuke fever. But I wasn't wacko. In fact, I felt fully sane—tingling, in control.*

I didn't need a shrink. I needed sanctuary.

And that's when the Pencil Theory hit me. I was sitting at my desk during the final hour of classes that day, daydreaming, doodling, and then bang, the answer was there like a gift from God. For a second I sat there frozen. I held the solution in my hand—a plain yellow pencil.

"Pencils," I said.

I must've said it in a loud voice, too loud, because the teacher suddenly jerked her head and gave me a long stare. I just smiled.

The rest was simple.

When the final bell rang, I trotted down to the school supply room, opened up my book bag, stuffed it full of No. 2 soft-lead pencils, zipped the bag shut, and hightailed it for home. Nothing to it. I didn't like the idea of thievery, but this wasn't a time for splitting moral hairs. It was a matter of live or die.

That evening, while my mom and dad were watching *I've Got a Secret*, I slipped down into the basement and quietly went to work reinforcing my shelter.

The theory was simple: Pencils contain lead; lead acts as an effective barrier against radiation.

It made perfect sense. Logical, scientific, practical.

Quickly, I stripped the table of everything I'd piled on it the night before, and then, very carefully, I began spreading out the pencils in neat rows, taking pains not to leave any cracks or spaces. Wizard, I thought. I replaced the lumber and bricks and rugs, added a double layer of charcoal briquettes, and then crowned it off with an old mattress. All told, my shelter's new roof was maybe three feet thick. More important, though, it now included that final defensive shield of solid lead.

Research Options

1. William builds a fallout shelter so that he'll be safe in the event of nuclear war. What are the pros and cons of his design? First, research the effects of nuclear war in the 1950s. Then determine whether William's fallout shelter would protect him from those effects. Share your conclusions with classmates.

2. As you learned in Chapter 18, some Americans did build backyard fallout shelters during the Cold War. Find different pictures—photographs, diagrams, advertisements—that illustrate what these fallout shelters looked like. To locate pictures, you might use resources such as history books about the Cold War in the 1950s and early 1960s, magazine articles from the time, or print or on-line encyclopedia articles. With your classmates, create a bulletin board display of fallout shelters and explain it to your classmates. Then, as a class, compare the real fallout shelters with William's.

CHAPTER **18**

Section 2

AMERICAN LIVES Douglas MacArthur
Flashy, Career Soldier

"When I joined the Army, even before the turn of the century, it was the fulfillment of all my boyish hopes and dreams."—Douglas MacArthur in his farewell address to Congress (1951)

Born to a Civil War hero and career officer, Douglas MacArthur grew up on military bases and spent almost his whole life in the Army. He was egotistical, a flashy dresser, and a self-promoter. Another officer once said that MacArthur's father "was the most flamboyantly egotistic man I had ever seen—until I met his son." MacArthur was also a superb officer—in the words of General George Marshall, "our most brilliant general."

MacArthur (1880–1964) succeeded through intelligence, hard work, and self-confidence instilled by his mother. As he prepared for the entrance exam for West Point, she told him, "You'll win if you don't lose your nerve. You must believe in yourself, my son, or no one else will believe in you." He outscored all competitors.

During World War I, MacArthur won a name for bravery in battle. He was also known for his non-regulation dress, which included a long scarf wrapped dashingly around his neck.

In 1935, he was loaned to the Philippines to build an army. MacArthur relished the chance to organize the force—and to design his own uniform—as field marshal in the Philippine army. In mid-1941, President Franklin Roosevelt recalled MacArthur to active duty and gave him command of U.S. forces in the Philippines.

MacArthur's troops were trapped when the Japanese attacked in late 1941. In March 1942, MacArthur and his troops managed to escape to Australia, thereby providing the American people with a hero when they needed one. MacArthur declared, "I came through, and I shall return." Characteristically, he did not say that "we"—the United States—would return.

It took two years, but MacArthur did return by pursuing an effective island-hopping strategy. He held casualties down by invading less-well-defended islands. He made effective use of bombers. Finally, in October 1944, U.S. forces landed on the Philippines. MacArthur bravely came ashore the same day and had his picture taken wading ashore. He told the Philippine people, "I have returned! . . . Rally to me!"

After the war, MacArthur led the American occupation of Japan. He helped demilitarize the country and his staff wrote a new constitution that included democratic reforms. The Japanese people appreciated his efforts.

When North Korea invaded the South in 1950, the situation was dire. MacArthur, placed in command of UN forces by President Harry Truman, planned a brilliant campaign—the invasion of Inchon, a port on the west side of the Korean peninsula behind enemy lines. Navy officers urged against it, as there were logistical problems with the landing site. At a meeting, MacArthur urged approval of the plan: "I can almost hear the ticking of the second hand of destiny. We must act now or we will die. . . . We shall land at Inchon and I shall crush them." The plan was adopted, and MacArthur was proven correct. American spirits soared as apparent defeat had turned to victory. However, MacArthur and President Truman began to disagree on war strategy, and MacArthur publicly disputed him. Then, in early 1951, just a few months after the Inchon landing, Truman shocked the nation by recalling—firing—MacArthur.

After Truman removed him from command, MacArthur was invited to speak before Congress and given a ticker-tape parade in New York. MacArthur hoped to run for president in 1952, but the Republicans turned to another general— Dwight Eisenhower. MacArthur lived the remainder of his life in uncharacteristic quiet.

Questions

1. What kind of image do you think MacArthur wanted to project?
2. MacArthur lived outside the United States from 1937 to 1951. What effect might that have had on his relations with Truman?
3. Why might Eisenhower have been more appealing as a presidential candidate than MacArthur?

CHAPTER 18

Section 3

AMERICAN LIVES Margaret Chase Smith
Independent Moderate

"Freedom of speech is not what it used to be in America. It has been so abused by some that it is not exercised by others." —Margaret Chase Smith in a Senate speech (1950)

Margaret Chase Smith (1897–1995) was an independent-minded Republican from Maine. The first woman to serve in both the House and the Senate, Smith spoke her mind and voted her beliefs—from 1940, when she supported Democratic President Franklin Roosevelt, to 1970, when she criticized Republican President Richard Nixon.

Margaret Chase began working as a teenager, even then showing her independence. "I didn't go to work because we were poor," she later recalled. "I went to work because I wanted to be independent. I wanted to spend my own money as I wanted to." Her jobs included work as a night telephone operator (at 10 cents an hour). Through this work, she met Clyde H. Smith, a politician.

By 1930, she had married Smith and entered local politics. She joined the Maine Republican Committee and became Smith's secretary when he was elected to Congress in 1936. Four years later, Smith died, and Margaret Chase Smith was elected to the seat. From the start, she followed her beliefs. In 1940, she voted for the Lend-Lease Act and the Selective Service Act, both positions counter to Republican policy but reflecting her interest in defense matters.

In 1948, Smith easily won election to the Senate. She served there until 1972 and eventually became senior Republican on the Armed Services and Aeronautical and Space Sciences committees.

In 1950, Smith realized that Senator Joe McCarthy had little evidence to back his charges about Communists in the government. Many were afraid to confront him, however. She wrote a "Declaration of Conscience" and persuaded six other Republican moderates to sign. On June 1, she spoke in the Senate against McCarthy. Then she read the declaration, which did not hesitate to criticize President Harry Truman for "lack of effective leadership" and "petty bitterness against" critics. But the declaration blasted "certain elements of the Republican Party" for "resorting to political smears." McCarthy rose from his seat and quietly left the chamber. Soon, though, he belittled Smith, her co-signers, and one other supporting senator as

"Snow White and the Seven Dwarfs."

McCarthy sought revenge in 1954. He sent a young supporter to run against Smith in the primary for her Senate seat. Smith trounced her opponent by a five-to-one margin. Her victory plus growing public disapproval of McCarthy convinced the Senate to censure him in 1954.

Smith took other independent stands in her career. She broke with Republican leadership in supporting federal aid to education, health insurance for older people, and some civil rights laws. Always in favor of a strong defense, Smith criticized President John F. Kennedy in 1961 for weakness in a summit with Soviet Premier Nikita Khrushchev. Once criticized by McCarthy, she was now attacked by Khrushchev, who called her "the devil in the disguise of a woman." In 1964, she became the first woman nominated for president by a major party, pulling 27 votes at the Republican convention.

In 1970 near the end of her Senate career—20 years after her stand against McCarthy—Smith once again urged moderation. Angered by the extremism of some of those protesting the Vietnam War, she lamented that "we have a national sickness now from which I pray we will recover." She also expressed anger at the Nixon administration for its overreaction to protesters.

Through all the years, Smith worked hard, setting a record for attending 2,941 straight Senate votes. Smith lost her re-election bid in 1972 and retired. She remained active into her nineties in charitable work as director of the Lily Endowment (1976–1992).

Questions

1. What stands did Margaret Chase Smith take against Republican Party positions?
2. What do you think Smith meant by the statement at the top of the page, which she made in her prelude to the "Declaration of Conscience"?
3. Compare Smith with her fellow senator Joseph McCarthy. Give three examples of some major differences between them.

CHAPTER
19
Section 1

GUIDED READING *Postwar America*

A. As you read this section, describe the solutions offered to deal with postwar problems.

1. Problem: Millions of veterans thrown out of work as they return to civilian life	
Solution offered by the Truman administration and Congress	

2. Problem: Severe housing shortage	
Solution offered by developers such as William Levitt	
Solutions offered by Congress under the Truman and Eisenhower administrations	

3. Problem: Runaway inflation	
Solution offered by the Truman administration and Congress	

4. Problem: Labor strikes that threaten to cripple the nation	
Solution offered by the Truman administration	

5. Problem: Discrimination and racial violence	
Solutions offered during the Truman administration	

B. On the back of this paper, explain the significance of **suburb, Dixiecrat,** and **Fair Deal.**

Name _____ Date _____

GUIDED READING *The American Dream in the Fifties*

A. As you read this section, write notes about how Americans were affected by various trends of the 1950s.

Trends	Effects
1. Business expansion: conglomerates and franchises	
2. Suburban expansion: flight from the cities	
3. Population growth: the baby boom	
4. Dramatic increase in leisure time	
5. Dramatic increase in the use of the automobile	
6. The rise of consumerism	

B. On the back of this paper, briefly explain **planned obsolescence.** Then tell how **Dr. Jonas Salk** affected American society in the 1950s.

CHAPTER 19

Section 3

GUIDED READING *Popular Culture*

A. As you read this section, take notes to answer questions about innovations and trends in 1950s popular culture.

1. Television	a. What are some of the most popular shows produced?	b. What kinds of subjects did television tend to present?	c. What kinds of subjects did it tend to avoid?
2. Radio	a. How did radio change to compete with television?	b. What role did it play in popularizing African-American culture?	
3. Film	How did movies change to compete with television?		
4. The beat movement	a. Who were the most famous beat writers?	b. What were the movement's chief characteristics?	
5. Rock 'n' roll	a. Who helped to popularize rock 'n' roll?	b. What were rock's chief characteristics?	

B. On the back of this paper, explain the purpose of the **Federal Communications Commission (FCC).**

Name _____ Date _____

A. As you read about problems faced by the "other" America of the 1950s, note some causes of each problem, solutions that were offered, and some effects of those solutions. (Notice that two answers have been provided for you.)

Problem: Decaying Cities		
1. Causes:	Solution offered: *Urban renewal*	2. Effects of solution:
Problem: Discrimination Against Mexican Americans		
Causes: *Prejudice against Hispanics;* *hard feelings toward braceros* *who stayed to work in the* *U.S. after World War II;* *illegal aliens escaping poor* *conditions in Mexico*	3. Solutions offered:	
Problem: Economic Hardship for Native Americans		
4. Causes:	5. Solutions offered:	6. Effects of solutions:

B. On the back of this paper, explain the terms **bracero** and **termination policy.**

Name _____ Date _____

BUILDING VOCABULARY *The Postwar Boom*

A. Matching Match the description in the second column with term in the first column. Write the appropriate letter next to the word.

_____ 1. braceros   a. attempt to improve a nation's inner cities

_____ 2. Fair Deal   b. Southern Democrats opposed to Truman

_____ 3. baby boom   c. company with many locations

_____ 4. consumerism   d. devised polio vaccine

_____ 5. Dr. Jonas Salk   e. Mexican hired hands in America

_____ 6. franchise   f. Truman's domestic program

_____ 7. Dixiecrats   g. rapid population growth after World War II

_____ 8. urban renewal   h. demand for material goods

B. Evaluating Write *T* in the blank if the statement is true. If the statement is false, write *F* in the blank and then write the corrected statement on the line below.

_____ 1. Under the termination policy, the federal government took greater responsibility for Native American tribes.

_____

_____ 2. The GI Bill of Rights provided free education and other forms of help to returning veterans.

_____

_____ 3. A conglomerate is a major corporation that includes a number of smaller companies in unrelated industries.

_____

_____ 4. The Federal Communications Commission was charged with regulating and licensing the travel industry.

_____

_____ 5. The communities that surrounding the nation's cities are called suburbs.

_____

C. Writing Write a paragraph describing the emergence of a youth subculture in the 1950s using the following terms.

CHAPTER

19

Section 3

SKILLBUILDER PRACTICE *Primary and Secondary Sources*

How did mainstream America in the 1950s react to rock 'n' roll? One way to find out is to look at the media reports of the time. Read this excerpt from a Time *magazine article, then answer the questions at the bottom of the page. (See Skillbuilder Handbook, p. R22.)*

In Boston, Roman Catholic leaders urged that the offensive music be boycotted. In Hartford, city officials considered revoking the State Theater's license after several audiences got too rowdy during a musical stage show. In Washington the police chief recommended banning such shows from the National Guard Armory after brawls in which several people were injured. In Minneapolis a theater manager withdrew a film featuring the music after a gang of youngsters left the theater, snake-danced around town and smashed windows. In Birmingham champions of white supremacy decried it as part of a Negro plot against the whites. At a wild concert in Atlanta's baseball park one night, fists and beer bottles were thrown, four youngsters were arrested.

The object of all this attention is a musical style known as "rock 'n' roll," which has captivated U.S. adolescents as swing captivated prewar teen-agers and ragtime vibrated those of the '20s. It does for music what a motorcycle club at full throttle does for a quiet Sunday afternoon.

Rock 'n' roll is based on Negro blues, but in a self-conscious style which underlines the primitive qualities of the blues with malice aforethought.

Characteristics: An unrelenting, socking syncopation that sounds like a bull whip; a choleric saxophone honking mating-call sounds; an electric guitar turned up so loud that its sound shatters and splits; a vocal group that shudders and exercises violently to the beat while roughly chanting either a near-nonsense phrase or a moronic lyric in hillbilly idiom.
Sample:

Long tall Sally has a lot on the ball
Nobody cares if she's long and tall
Oh, Baby! Yeh-heh-heh-hes, Baby
Whoo-oo-oo-oo, Baby! I'm havin' me
*   some fun tonight, yeah. . . .*

Does rock-'n'-roll music itself encourage any form of juvenile delinquency? . . . Pop Record Maker Mitch Miller, no rock 'n' roller, sums up for the defense: "You can't call any music immoral. If anything is wrong with rock 'n' roll, it is that it makes a virtue out of monotony." For the prosecution, the best comment comes indirectly from Actress Judy Holliday in *Born Yesterday:* It's just not couth, that's all.

from *Time* (June 18, 1956), 54.

1. What is the source of this information? _____

2. Is the source qualified to report on this subject? Explain. _____

_____

3. What is the tone of the article?_____

_____

4. Are there more statements of fact or of opinion? Underline all statements of opinion in the article.

_____

5. Would this be a good source of information about attitudes toward rock 'n' roll in the '50s? Explain.

_____

_____

CHAPTER
19
Section 1

RETEACHING ACTIVITY *Postwar America*

Finding Main Ideas

The following questions deal with events on the home front during World War II. Answer them in the space provided.

1. What factors were behind the country's post war economic boom?

_____

_____

2. How did President Truman advance the cause of civil rights?

_____

_____

3. How did midterm elections of 1946 have an unfavorable impact on organized labor?

_____

_____

4. Why did President Truman refer to the 80th Congress as "do-nothing"?

_____

_____

5. In what ways did Truman's New Deal meet with mixed results?

_____

_____

6. What was President Eisenhower's "dynamic conservatism" approach?

_____

_____

CHAPTER
19
Section 2

RETEACHING ACTIVITY *The American Dream in the Fifties*

Reading Comprehension

The statements below are headlines that could have been written during the 1950s.
In the space provided write several sentences that support each headline with
specific details.

1. America Becomes Home to the Organization and Organization Man

_____

_____

_____

_____

2. A New Suburban Lifestyle Takes Hold

_____

_____

_____

_____

3. An Automobile Culture Emerges

_____

_____

_____

_____

4. Consumerism Abounds in America

_____

_____

_____

_____

CHAPTER

19

RETEACHING ACTIVITY *Popular Culture*

Section 3

A. Matching

Match the description in the second column with the person in the first column.
Write the appropriate letter next to the word.

_____ 1. Allen Ginsburg   a. called television a "vast wasteland"

_____ 2. Miles Davis   b. unofficial "King of Rock 'n' Roll"

_____ 3. Jack Kerouac   c. prominent beat poet

_____ 4. James Dean   d. innovative jazz artist

_____ 5. Elvis Presley   e. popular fifties movie star

_____ 6. Newton Minow   f. wrote beat novel *On the Road*

B. Completion

Complete each sentence with the appropriate term or name.

television	beats
racism	African Americans
western	conformity
Asian Americans	poverty

1. For the most part, television in the 1950s omitted references to controversial issues, such as
   _____ and _____.

2. Rock 'n' roll owes much of its sound to earlier music performed by _____.

3. By 1960, a _____ could be found in nearly 90 percent of American homes.

4. Members of the beat movement rebelled against what they viewed as too much _____ in
   America.

5. One popular genre of the early television was the _____.

CHAPTER 19
Section 4

RETEACHING ACTIVITY *The Other America*

Reading Comprehension

Choose the best answer for each item. Write the letter of your answer in the blank.

_____ 1. "White flight" involved the mass exodus of white Americans from the nation's
  a. cities.
  b. suburbs.
  c. farms.
  d. coast lines.

_____ 2. The author of the influential book *The Other America: Poverty in the United States* was
  a. James Dean.
  b. Jack Kerouac.
  c. Michael Harrington.
  d. Felix Longoria.

_____ 3. *Braceros* were workers who came to the United States from
  a. Europe.
  b. Asia.
  c. Mexico.
  d. Africa.

_____ 4. The Longoria incident involved the refusal by town officials to provide funeral services for a World War II veteran because he was
  a. African American.
  b. Mexican-American.
  c. Japanese-American.
  d. Native American.

_____ 5. The unsuccessful effort to assimilate Native Americans by moving them off their reservations and into the nation's cities was known as the
  a. termination policy.
  b. Dawes Act.
  c. *bracero* program.
  d. Indian Reorganization Act.

_____ 6. The nation's poor in the 1950s were found in large numbers in every group except
  a. the elderly.
  b. single women.
  c. minorities.
  d. suburban residents.

GEOGRAPHY APPLICATION: HUMAN–ENVIRONMENT INTERACTION

The Baby Boom

CHAPTER 19

Section 2

Directions: Read the paragraphs below and study the graph carefully. Then answer the questions that follow.

The term *baby boom* refers to the years 1946 to 1964 when the population of the United States soared due to a dramatic postwar increase in the annual birthrate. The birthrate had been declining fairly steadily for decades, falling below 20 births per 1,000 people for the first time in 1931. In 1941, however, the birthrate edged back up over 20 and stayed above that figure through 1964.

At the height of the baby boom, from 1954 to 1961, more than 4 million babies were born in the Unites States every year. Many women who might have stayed childless at other times decided to have children. One sociologist wrote about the "pro-child social values" that characterized the period: "Those who didn't want children were an embarrassed and embattled minority. It [not having children] was almost evidence of a physical or mental deficiency."

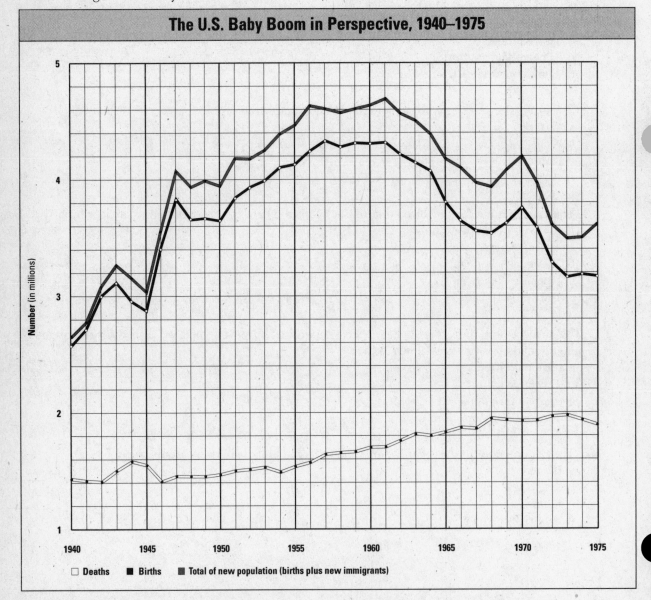

The U.S. Baby Boom in Perspective, 1940–1975

□ Deaths   ■ Births   ▪ Total of new population (births plus new immigrants)

Interpreting Text and Visuals

1. What happened to the number of births in the two years prior to 1946? _____

2. What was probably the major cause of the beginning of the baby boom? _____

   _____

   _____

3. Look at the graph's 1959 totals. What does the 4.30 level indicate? _____

   What does the level of 4.60 indicate? _____

   What does the level of 1.66 indicate? _____

   By how much did the U.S. population increase in that year? _____

4. Nearly 60,000 more people immigrated to the United States in 1965 than in 1964.
   Why then does the top line in the graph dip down between those years? _____

   _____

   _____

5. What is significant about the number of births in 1972? (Hint: Look at the
   number of births for the first year of the baby boom.) _____

   _____

   Why do you think 1964 is considered the final year of the baby boom? _____

   _____

   _____

   _____

6. Contrast the patterns of births and deaths during the years 1940–1975. _____

   _____

   _____

   _____

PRIMARY SOURCE Cartoon

This cartoon spoofs the housing developments of the 1950s that gave Americans the cookie-cutter homes and neighborhoods they craved. According to the cartoon, what was one negative aspect of postwar suburban developments?

CHAPTER
19
Section 1

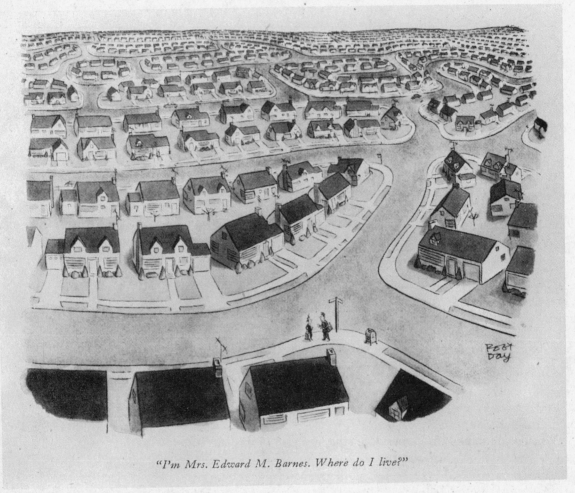

"I'm Mrs. Edward M. Barnes. Where do I live?"

Discussion Questions

1. What words or phrases would you use to describe the housing development depicted in this cartoon?
2. How do you think the woman in the cartoon, Mrs. Edward M. Barnes, feels about living in a suburban development?

3. Why do you think Americans in the 1950s wanted to live in a housing development like this one? Cite evidence from your textbook to support your opinion.

PRIMARY SOURCE *from The Organization Man*

Through the "looking glass" of the typical suburban community of Park Forest, Illinois, William H. Whyte, Jr., examined 1950s beliefs and values. As you read this excerpt from Whyte's study, think about his concept of the organization man.

This book is about the organization man. If the term is vague, it is because I can think of no other way to describe the people I am talking about. They are not the workers, nor are they the white-collar people in the usual, clerk sense of the word. These people only work for The Organization. The ones I am talking about *belong* to it as well. They are the ones of our middle class who have left home, spiritually as well as physically, to take the vows of organization life, and it is they who are the mind and soul of our great self-perpetuating institutions. Only a few are top managers or ever will be. In a system that makes such hazy terminology as "junior executive" psychologically necessary, they are of the staff as much as the line, and most are destined to live poised in a middle area that still awaits satisfactory euphemism. . . .

The corporation man is the most conspicuous example, but he is only one, for the collectivization so visible in the corporation has affected almost every field of work. Blood brother to the business trainee off to join Du Pont is the seminary student who will end up in the church hierarchy, the doctor headed for the corporate clinic, the physics Ph.D. in a government laboratory, the intellectual on the foundation-sponsored team project, the engineering graduate in the huge drafting room at Lockheed, the young apprentice in a Wall Street law factory.

They are all, as they so often put it, in the same boat. Listen to them talk to each other over the front lawns of their suburbia and you cannot help but be struck by how well they grasp the common denominators which bind them. Whatever the differences in their organization ties, it is the common problems of collective work that dominate their attentions, and when the Du Pont man talks to the research chemist or the chemist to the army man, it is these problems that are uppermost. The word *collective* most of them can't bring themselves to use—except to describe foreign countries or organizations they don't work for—but they are keenly aware of how much more deeply beholden they are to organization than were their elders. They are wry about it, to be sure; they talk of the "treadmill," the "rat race," of the inability to control one's direction. But they have no

great sense of plight; between themselves and organization they believe they see an ultimate harmony. . . .

[My concern in this book] is the principle impact that organization life has had on the individuals within it. A collision has been taking place—indeed, hundreds of thousands of them, and in the aggregate they have been producing what I believe is a major shift in American ideology.

Officially, we are a people who hold to the Protestant Ethic. . . . [T]here is almost always the thought that pursuit of individual salvation through hard work, thrift, and competitive struggle is the heart of the American achievement.

But the harsh facts of organization life simply do not jibe with these precepts. This conflict is certainly not a peculiarly American development. . . .

It is in America, however, that the contrast between the old ethic and current reality has been most apparent—and most poignant. Of all peoples it is we who have led in the public worship of individualism. . . . We kept on, and as late as the twenties, when big organization was long since a fact, affirmed the old faith as if nothing had really changed at all.

Today many still try, and it is the members of the kind of organization most responsible for the change, the corporation, who try the hardest. It is the corporation man [who] . . . honestly wants to believe he follows the tenets he extols, and if he extols them so frequently it is, perhaps, to shut out a nagging suspicion that he, too, the last defender of the faith, is no longer pure. Only by using the language of individualism to describe the collective can he stave off the thought that he himself is in a collective.

from William H. Whyte, Jr., *The Organization Man* (New York: Simon and Schuster, 1956), 3–5.

Discussion Questions

1. What characteristics defined an organization man?
2. What conflict does Whyte see between the American value of individualism and the fact of organization life?
3. Do you think the conflict Whyte identifies for the 1950s still exists today? Explain.

CHAPTER 19

Section 4

PRIMARY SOURCE *from* The Other America

Sociologist Michael Harrington studied the plight of the "invisible" poor. His shock-ing report spurred Presidents John F. Kennedy and Lyndon B. Johnson to fight the War on Poverty. As you read this excerpt from Harrington's study, compare "other" Americans with those who realized the American dream in the 1950s.

There is a familiar America. It is celebrated in speeches and advertised on television and in the magazines. It has the highest mass standard of living the world has ever known.

In the 1950s this America worried about itself, yet even its anxieties were products of abundance. The title of a brilliant book [John Kenneth Galbraith's *The Affluent Society*] was widely misin-terpreted, and the familiar America began to call itself "the affluent society." There was introspection about Madison Avenue and tail fins; there was dis-cussion of the emotional suffering taking place in the suburbs. In all this, there was an implicit assumption that the basic grinding economic prob-lems had been solved in the United States. In this theory the nation's problems were no longer a mat-ter of basic human needs, of food, shelter, and clothing. Now they were seen as qualitative, a ques-tion of learning to live decently amid luxury.

While this discussion was carried on, there existed another America. In it dwelt somewhere between 40,000,000 and 50,000,000 citizens of this land. They were poor. They still are.

To be sure, the other America is not impover-ished in the same sense as those poor nations where millions cling to hunger as a defense against starva-tion. This country has escaped such extremes. That does not change the fact that tens of millions of Americans are, at this very moment, maimed in body and spirit, existing at levels beneath those necessary for human decency. If these people are not starving, they are hungry, and sometimes fat with hunger, for that is what cheap foods do. They are without ade-quate housing and education and medical care.

The Government has documented what this means to the bodies of the poor, and the figures will be cited throughout this book. But even more basic, this poverty twists and deforms the spirit. The American poor are pessimistic and defeated, and they are victimized by mental suffering to a degree unknown in Suburbia.

This book is a description of the world in which these people live; it is about the other America.

Here are the unskilled workers, the migrant farm workers, the aged, the minorities, and all the others who live in the economic underworld of American life. In all this, there will be statistics, and that offers the opportunity for disagreement among honest and sincere men. I would ask the reader to respond critically to every assertion, but not to allow statistical quibbling to obscure the huge, enormous, and intolerable fact of poverty in America. For, when all is said and done, that fact is unmistakable, whatever its exact dimensions, and the truly human reaction can only be outrage. . . .

There are perennial reasons that make the other America an invisible land.

Poverty is often off the beaten track. It always has been. The ordinary tourist never left the main highway, and today he rides interstate turnpikes. He does not go into the valleys of Pennsylvania where the towns look like the movie sets of Wales in the thirties. He does not see the company houses in rows, the rutted roads (the poor always have bad roads whether they live in the city, in towns, or on farms), and everything is black and dirty. And even if he were to pass through such a place by accident, the tourist would not meet the unemployed men in the bar or the women coming home from a run-away sweatshop.

from Michael Harrington, *The Other America: Poverty in the United States* (Baltimore: Penguin Books, 1962), 9–11.

Research Options

1. According to Harrington's study, 40 to 50 million Americans were poor in the 1950s. Use a resource such as *The World Almanac and Book of Facts* to find out how many Americans are poor today. Has the number of poor people in the United States increased or decreased since the 1950s?

2. Research the government programs that were initiated under the Kennedy and Johnson administrations to help the poor in the United States. Then make a chart to share your findings.

CHAPTER
19

Section 4

PRIMARY SOURCE The Voluntary
Relocation Program

*During the 1950s and 1960s, the federal government's Bureau of Indian Affairs sub-
sidized the resettlement of some 35,000 rural Native Americans in urban areas. This
voluntary relocation program, begun in response to the federal government's plan
to "terminate" the tribes, ultimately failed. Native Americans encountered discrimination and a lack of adequate housing and jobs. As Watt Spade and Willard Walker
indicate in their account of a visit to Chicago in this period, many of those who
moved to the cities did not choose to stay.*

One time I went up there to Chicago where my
brother lives. Rabbit is his name. He was right
there when I got off the bus. We were a little hungry
so we stopped to eat on the way across town. This
restaurant we stopped at was all glass on the outside,
like one big window. You could see all the people
eating inside. They weren't sitting down either; they
were all standing up at a counter that wound all
around through the place. They were standing along
both sides of this counter, but they didn't seem to be
talking to each other or looking at each other. It was
like they were all looking at the wall.

My brother and I decided to eat at a place called
Wally's Bar over near where he lives at Fullerton
and Green. There were a lot of people in that place
and they were all very friendly. They all seemed to
know my brother too, but they called him "Indian
Joe." I hadn't ever heard him called that.

Rabbit told me he didn't have any place where I
could stay. He had an apartment, but they'd had a
fire there a few days before. We went over to look
at it, and I guess he hadn't been there for a few
days because there was a letter from Momma on
the stairs right where you come in. There was black
soot on the stairs all the way up to the fourth floor,
where his apartment was; and there were some
Puerto Rican guys up there cleaning the place up.
They had the radio turned on real loud playing
some kind of Puerto Rican music. The whole place
smelled like charcoal and burnt furniture.

We went back to that place where they all
called Rabbit "Indian Joe" and I told him about the
news from home. Then he told me all about the

city and about Chicago Rawhide, where he works.
Finally I said I didn't think I was ready to settle
down there just yet. We went on back to the bus
station and waited around for the bus back to
Oklahoma. There were a couple of Indian guys
there, and they were telling this story. They said
the government wanted to put a man on the moon
and it could be done alright, but nobody knew how
to get the guy home again after he landed on the
moon. These guys said all the government had to
do was put an Indian in that rocket ship and tell
him he was being relocated and then, after he got
to the moon, that Indian would find his own way
home again and the government wouldn't have to
figure that part out at all.

Rabbit and I sure liked that story. I wonder
what ever happened to those two Indian guys.

from "Relocation" in *Cherokee Stories* by the Reverend
Watt Spade and Willard Walker (Middletown: Wesleyan
University Laboratory of Anthropology, 1966).

Discussion Questions

1. What were the narrator's first impressions of
   Chicago after he arrived by bus from Oklahoma?
2. What kind of life did Rabbit lead in Chicago?
3. Why do you think the narrator decided not to
   stay in Chicago with his brother?
4. Think about the story that the two Native
   Americans told at the bus station. Does the story
   reflect the success or the failure of the voluntary
   relocation program? Explain your response.

CHAPTER 19

Section 2

LITERATURE SELECTION *from* **The Man in the Gray Flannel Suit** by Sloan Wilson

Tom Rath, the main character of this novel, married Betsy when he was 21 and then served as a paratrooper during World War II. After the war, the Raths settled down to life in a Connecticut suburb; Tom commutes to his job in Manhattan, while Betsy stays at home to raise their three children. As you read this excerpt, think about how the Raths feel about the pursuit of the American dream.

By the time they had lived seven years in the little house on Greentree Avenue in Westport, Connecticut, they both detested it. There were many reasons, none of them logical, but all of them compelling. For one thing, the house had a kind of evil genius for displaying proof of their weaknesses and wiping out all traces of their strengths. The ragged lawn and weed-filled garden proclaimed to passers-by and the neighbors that Thomas R. Rath and his family disliked "working around the place" and couldn't afford to pay someone else to do it. The interior of the house was even more vengeful. In the living room there was a big dent in the plaster near the floor, with a huge crack curving up from it in the shape of a question mark. That wall was damaged in the fall of 1952, when, after struggling for months to pay up the back bills, Tom came home one night to find that Betsy had bought a cut-glass vase for forty dollars. Such an extravagant gesture was utterly unlike her, at least since the war. Betsy was a conscientious household manager, and usually when she did something Tom didn't like, they talked the matter over with careful reasonableness. But on that particular night, Tom was tired and worried because he himself had just spent seventy dollars on a new suit he felt he needed to dress properly for his business, and at the climax of a heated argument, he picked up the vase and heaved it against the wall. The heavy glass shattered, the plaster cracked, and two of the laths behind it broke. The next morning, Tom and Betsy worked together on their knees to patch the plaster, and they repainted the whole wall, but when the paint dried, the big dent near the floor with the crack curving up from it almost to the ceiling in the

> **The crack remained as a perpetual reminder of Betsy's moment of extravagance, Tom's moment of violence, and their inability either to fix walls properly or to pay to have them fixed.**

shape of a question mark was still clearly visible. The fact that the crack was in the shape of a question mark did not seem symbolic to Tom and Betsy, nor even amusing—it was just annoying. Its peculiar shape caused people to stare at it abstractly, and once at a cocktail party one of the guests said, "Say, that's funny. Did you ever notice that big question mark on your wall?"

"It's only a crack," Tom replied.

"But why should it be in the form of a question mark?"

"It's just coincidence."

"That's funny," the guest said. Tom and Betsy assured each other that someday they would have the whole wall replastered, but they never did. The crack remained as a perpetual reminder of Betsy's moment of extravagance, Tom's moment of violence, and their inability either to fix walls properly or to pay to have them fixed. It seemed ironic to Tom that the house should preserve a souvenir of such things, while allowing evenings of pleasure and kindness to slip by without a trace.

The crack in the living room was not the only reminder of the worst. An ink stain with hand marks on the wallpaper in Janey's room commemorated one of the few times Janey ever willfully destroyed property, and the only time Betsy ever lost her temper with her and struck her. Janey was five, and the middle one of the three Rath children. She did everything hard: she screamed when she cried, and when she was happy her small face seemed to hold for an instant all the joy in the world. Upon deciding that she wanted to play with ink, she carefully poured ink over both her hands and made neat imprints on the wallpaper, from the floor to as high as she could reach. Betsy was so angry that she slapped both her hands, and Janey, feeling she had simply been interrupted in the midst of an artistic endeavor, lay on the bed for an hour sobbing and rubbing her hands in her eyes until her whole face was covered with ink. Feeling like a murderess, Betsy tried to comfort her, but even holding and rocking her didn't seem to help, and Betsy was shocked to find that the child was shuddering. When Tom came home that night he found mother and daughter asleep on the bed together, tightly locked in each other's arms. Both their faces were covered with ink. All this the wall remembered and recorded.

A thousand petty shabbinesses bore witness to the negligence of the Raths. The front door had been scratched by a dog which had been run over the year before. The hot-water faucet in the bathroom dripped. Almost all the furniture needed to be refinished, reuphol-stered, or cleaned. And besides that, the house was too small, ugly, and almost precisely like the houses on all sides of it. The Raths had bought the house in 1946, shortly after Tom had got out of the army and, at the suggestion of his grandmother, become an assistant to the director of the Schanenhauser Foundation, an organization which an elderly millionaire had established to help finance scientific research and the arts. They had told each other that they probably would be in the house only one or two years before they could afford something better. It took them five years to realize that the expense of raising three children was likely to increase as fast as Tom's salary at a charitable foundation. If Tom and Betsy had been entirely reasonable, this might have caused them to start painting the place like crazy, but it had the reverse effect. Without talking about it much, they both began to think of the house as a trap, and they no more enjoyed refurbishing it than a prisoner would delight in shining up the bars of his cell. Both of them were aware that their feelings about the house were not admirable.

"I don't know what's the matter with us," Betsy said one night. "Your job is plenty good enough. We've got three nice kids, and lots of people would be glad to have a house like this. We shouldn't be so *discontented* all the time."

"Of course we shouldn't!" Tom said.

> *"I don't know what's the matter with us," Betsy said one night. . . . "We shouldn't be so discontented all the time."*

Their words sounded hollow. It was curious to believe that that house with the crack in the form of a question mark on the wall and the ink stains on the wallpaper was probably the end of their personal road. It was impossible to believe. Somehow something would have to happen.

Tom thought about his house on that day early in June 1953, when a friend of his named Bill Hawthorne mentioned the possibility of a job at the United Broadcasting Corporation. Tom was having lunch with a group of acquaintances in The Golden Horseshoe, a small restaurant and bar near Rockefeller Center.

"I hear we've got a new spot opening up in our public-relations department," Bill who wrote promotion for United Broadcasting said. "I think any of you would be crazy to take it, mind you, but if you're interested, there it is. . . ."

Tom unfolded his long legs under the table and shifted his big body on his chair restlessly. "How much would it pay?" he asked casually.

"I don't know," Bill said. "Anywhere from eight to twelve thousand, I'd guess, according to how good a hold-up man you are. If you try for it, ask fifteen. I'd like to see somebody stick the bastards good."

It was fashionable that summer to be cynical about one's employers, and the promotion men were the most cynical of all.

"You can have it," Cliff Otis, a young copy-writer for a large advertising agency, said. "I wouldn't want to get into a rat race like that."

Tom glanced into his glass and said nothing. Maybe I could get ten thousand a year, he thought. If I could do that, Betsy and I might be able to buy a better house.

Discussion Questions

1. What condition is the Raths' house in?
2. What is their attitude toward the house after they have lived there for seven years?
3. Betsy Rath does not understand why they are not satisfied with what they have, why they are so discontented. What do you think is their problem?
4. Do you think the Raths' problem is characteristic only of the post-World War II era, or is it characteristic of other times as well? Explain.

CHAPTER 19

Section 3

LITERATURE SELECTION *from 1959*
by Thulani Davis

Set in the South, 1959 is narrated by a 12-year-old African-American girl named Willie Tarrant. As you read this excerpt from the novel, pay attention to aspects of late '50s popular culture such as fashion, music, dances, and TV programs.

That evening [my brother] Preston shined his loafers with the tassels, slapped on the Aqua Velva, left the collar button open on his shirt, and split before anyone could find out where he was headed. Naturally I had to wonder if he'd gone over to Ulysses Grant Street, yet I was inclined to dismiss the whole idea. It was obvious, first of all, that he was too young for Cassie. On the other hand, Preston was cute, in the pretty-boy way. But then he dressed like a college kid, not like the slick pretty boys with their high-waters, tight black socks, and close-cut hair with the part on the side. Jack Dempsey had been more like them, even though he wasn't skinny like most of the cool boys. They didn't go out for athletics—they went in for wine.

When he'd left, I went in his room to play some 45s. I laid the Elvis Presleys to the side—that was his stuff. I stuck pretty strictly to the old and fast ones. "I'm searchin' . . . searchin' every whiiiitcha way . . ." Actually, Jack Dempsey had been really cool. It was obvious Cassie would have liked him, everybody did. She must be heartbroken. I'd seen him outside the high school, even in the paper. He had a *Quo Vadis* cut and wore a black leather over his varsity sweaters. And even though I thought Preston could be cool, he was still Preston, too nice to be really cool. He wasn't ever going to be really cool, just like I knew I wouldn't ever really be cool. Too straight. And as for me, there was just too much stuff I didn't know. I was always late on the pickup. . . .

Preston's record collection wasn't keeping up. He hadn't gotten my new song, "Personality." I could pull it out at the record store and take it in the booth and listen to it, but I almost never had money when I got to go down there. The Coasters and Chuck Willis would do. I practiced the stroll back and forth to "Betty and Dupree" in his room. Everybody had been doing the slop, but this new line dance was on TV, and now it was the thing. Black kids made the stroll look colored, better than on *Bandstand*. We put an easy rock on it, like a walk with a dip, casual—the same as we did with all the dances. . . .

Saturday was dedication day on WRAP—Rrrap Radio—and we had put the radios on in the living room and our bedrooms. The colored station was nonstop, rapid-fire jokes, plus a lot of commentary from the DJs on why they were great. On Sundays, though, we listened to the white stations because WRAP did church from can-do to can't. That involved a lot of dial flipping because the other stations only played r&b every tenth song. Every Sunday I counted to see if they would ever play more than two an hour, or even two an hour twice in a row.

Fat Freddie was running his mouth and reading out the plays. All the Busters and Judys and Cookies and Marvins were on the waves in love. Preston and I could never understand how come we never knew any of them. Of course, Preston maintained he was too cool to call in to a radio show. All the same, with all the Negro kids going to three schools, it seemed as though we should at least have *heard* of anybody calling in. Just how many colored kids were out there anyway? We made the old man keep it on in the car. If we did hear some familiar names, it would be something to talk about.

Activity Options

1. Rewrite this passage, giving it a 21st-century twist. Use contemporary references to popular culture instead of references to 1950s clothes, music, dance, and so forth. Then read your passage aloud to classmates.
2. Listen to music by performers who were popular in the fifties, including Elvis Presley, the Coasters, and Chuck Willis. Discuss with your classmates some of the similarities and differences between '50s music and popular music today.
3. Find out how to do the stroll, the slop, or another dance that was popular in the 1950s and then demonstrate it for the class.

CHAPTER 19

Section 1

AMERICAN LIVES **Jackie Robinson**
Driven to Break Barriers

"There were [in 1949] other blacks in baseball—and we suffered much abuse ourselves—but [Jackie] was still the man who integrated baseball, and he lived under more pressure than any human being I met in my life (and that includes Martin Luther King, Jr.)."—former Dodger teammate Don Newcombe (1994)

All his life, Jackie Robinson struggled to break down racial barriers. In 1947, he did so in a spectacular way by becoming the first African American to play major-league baseball. His will to win baseball games made him one of the top stars of the sport.

Robinson (1919–1972) was a star athlete in high school and college, where he excelled in seven sports. When World War II broke out, he entered the army. He applied for officer training school but was refused because of his race. Robinson protested the injustice and won: he and other African Americans were admitted to the school. Later in his army career, he refused to move to the back of a bus simply because he was black. He was court-martialed but acquitted.

After the war, Robinson began to play professional baseball. However, he played for a team in the Negro Leagues, because regular major-league baseball had a ban on African-American players. At about this time, though, Branch Rickey, co-owner of the Brooklyn Dodgers, decided to end that ban, and he started looking for just the right African-American ballplayer to break the color line. He had to be talented, with a background beyond criticism—including smoking and drinking. He had to have unshakable self-control. He had to have a "must-win" attitude. Rickey felt that Jackie Robinson would be ideal—if he would take the responsibility.

Rickey asked for a meeting with Robinson. To test Robinson's response to what he would hear from fans and opposing players, Rickey heaped verbal abuse and confrontations on him for nearly three hours. Robinson finally asked Rickey if he wanted "a ballplayer who's afraid to fight back." Rickey answered, "I want a player with guts enough not to fight back." Robinson accepted the terms and promised there would be no incidents. Rickey then signed him to play second base for the 1946 season with the Montreal Royals, a Dodgers team in the International League.

Robinson's performance in the minor leagues was sensational. He had the highest batting average in the league and led his team to the Junior World Series Championship.

In 1947, Robinson joined the Dodgers. Throughout the season, he endured hate mail and threats from strangers, foul names and taunts from fans, and close pitches and hard slides from opponents. Remembering his promise, he responded simply by outplaying his opponents. With timely hitting, bold baserunning, and steady fielding, he became a leader. Some of his teammates were reluctant to play with him at first. However, his talents changed their minds. As one recalled, he was accepted "because everybody wanted to win." Win they did. Robinson helped lead the Dodgers to a National League pennant in 1947 and won baseball's award as rookie of the year.

Robinson continued to play winning baseball. Daring baserunning was his trademark. Nineteen times he stole home, a difficult feat. In ten years, he led the Dodgers to six league pennants and a world championship.

Robinson retired in 1957, and in 1962 he was voted into the Baseball Hall of Fame. He died from complications of high blood pressure and diabetes at age 53, a few weeks after his uniform number was retired by the Dodgers, now based in Los Angeles. As a tribute for the 50th anniversary of his milestone, major-league baseball dedicated its 1997 season to Robinson. All players and umpires wore a "Breaking Barriers" arm patch, and all teams used special baseballs with the commemorative logo in their home openers.

Questions

1. Many people agree that Robinson was not the best player in the Negro League in the mid-1940s. If so, why did Rickey choose him?
2. Do you think professional sports would be the same today if it had not been for Robinson?
3. Do you think Robinson's success with the Dodgers had any impact beyond sports?

CHAPTER
19

Section 3

AMERICAN LIVES # Milton Berle
The Rise and Fall of a Television Star

"In a sense, [the comedy-variety television show] all goes back to Berle."
—Variety *magazine (1958)*

Milton Berle has spent almost his entire life in show business. A wild comedian known for his crazy visual humor, he became famous as the first major star of television. However, his star fell almost as quickly as it rose, and to people under forty, he is virtually an unknown name today.

Born in 1908, Berle was entertaining people in his New York City neighborhood as a five-year-old. He soon appeared in movies and became part of a vaudeville act. Vaudeville was a popular stage entertainment that thrived from about 1900 to the 1920s. It combined singing, dancing girls, and rowdy comedians. Comedy became Berle's life. He told jokes. He wore funny costumes. He took a fall or had someone in the cast throw a pie in his face. As long as it got a laugh, Berle would do it.

He became a headliner—the top draw in the roster of acts in a vaudeville show. He also became the master of ceremonies at New York's Palace Theater, the most famous vaudeville house of all. Often, when he heard another comedian's funny line, he used it in his own act. For his habit of taking other people's material, he was called "The Thief of Bad Gags," a pun on *The Thief of Baghdad,* a popular movie of the day.

Starting in the late 1920s, radio became a popular mass entertainment. Berle tried to take advantage of the new medium. He had six different shows, searching for a formula that would work. However, while a studio audience might laugh uproariously at his craziness on stage, people at home, of course, could not see what he was doing. Each show was canceled.

In the late 1940s, Berle got another chance. He sensed that television was the perfect vehicle, giving the home audience the chance to see his gags. In 1948 he signed to host a variety show. That year he rotated with six other hosts, but his physical humor attracted viewers like nobody else. More than 90 percent of all homes with a television set watched when he was host. At the time, those homes were still very few—only 1 percent of the

country. Berle, though, helped change that. Sales of television sets shot up—200,000 a month in 1948 and 1949.

In 1949, Berle became the sole host of the show. *Variety* magazine, which reports on the entertainment industry, said that on Tuesday nights, when Berle's show was broadcast, attendance at theaters and night clubs dropped. Berle was hailed as "Mr. Television." *Time* and *Newsweek* both did cover stories about him. Fearing he might go elsewhere, his network signed him to a contract for 30 years.

However, just as quickly, Berle's popularity fell. At first televisions were owned mostly by people living in cities in the East and Midwest. More and more, in the early 1950s, television owners lived in the South and West and in rural areas. Berle's humor had less appeal to them. They found his insider jokes about New York City unfunny. Also, his loud pranks grew stale. As another early television star later noted, "I don't care who you are. Finally you'll get on people's nerves if they get too much of you." So, Berle's ratings slipped. He fell to third place in the 1951–1952 season and did not even reach the top ten in 1954–1955. Within a couple years, he was off the air. Two attempts to revive his show failed.

Though his show had ended, Berle kept on entertaining. He appeared on variety shows and situation comedies and even acted in dramatic roles—one time winning an Emmy award. He made a few movies in the 1970s and 1980s and continued to work night clubs. In the 1990s he has only rarely appeared on television—mostly at celebrity roasts and award shows.

Questions

1. Why did Berle not succeed in radio?
2. What two factors led to Berle's declining popularity on television?
3. What does the rise and fall of Berle's career suggest about celebrity?

Answer Key

Chapter 16, Section 1
GUIDED READING

A. Possible answers:

1. Stalin: Soviet Union

   Political: communism; strengthen communism in the Soviet Union; the spread of communism by worker's revolutions throughout the world; state ownership of property; eventual rule by the working class

   Actions: massive campaigns to collectivize agriculture and to industrialize the nation; the Great Purge

2. Mussolini: Italy

   Political: fascism; extreme nationalism; militaristic expansionism; private property; a strong centralized government; anti-communism

   Actions: the "march on Rome"; the Rome-Berlin Axis Pact; the invasion of Ethiopia

3. Hitler: Germany

   Political: Nazism; extreme nationalism and racism; militaristic expansionism; private property; a strong government; anti-communism

   Actions: established the Third Reich; pulled out of the League of Nations; built up the military; sent troops into the Rhineland; set up the Rome-Berlin Axis Pact

4. Militarists: Japan

   Political: nationalism; militaristic expansionism

   Actions: the invasion of Manchuria; pulled out of the League of Nations

5. Franco: Spain

   Political: fascism; militarism

   Actions: an uprising against the elected government; a civil war

B. Answers will vary widely depending upon the specifics noted.

Chapter 16, Section 2
GUIDED READING

A. Possible answers:

1. To avoid war

2. The pact was dishonorable and wouldn't prevent war.

3. Not to fight each other; to divide Poland between them

4. Poland was divided between Germany and the USSR; the country ceased to exist; Britain and France declared war on Germany.

5. Germany occupied the northern part of France; a Nazi-controlled puppet government was set up at Vichy in Southern France.

6. Air war; a British victory forced Hitler to call off the invasion of Britain indefinitely.

B. Answers will vary widely depending upon the specifics noted.

Chapter 16, Section 3
GUIDED READING

A. Possible answers:

1. Worried about fueling anti-Semitism; didn't want more

2. Stripped Jews of their civil rights and property if they tried to leave Germany; forced Jews to wear Jewish stars sewn to their clothing

3. Gangs of Nazi storm troopers attacked Jewish homes, businesses, and synagogues.

4. Widespread anti-Semitism; desire to avoid greater competition for jobs during the Depression; fear of "enemy agents"

5. All non-Aryans; Jews; Communists; socialists; liberals; gypsies; Freemasons; Jehovah's Witnesses; homosexuals; the mentally retarded; the insane; the disabled; the incurably ill; Poles; Ukrainians; Russians

6. The Nazis shot, beat, starved, gassed, and hanged their victims; they also worked them to death, injected them with poison, and deliberately killed them in grisly "medical" experiments.

B. Answers will vary depending upon the specifics noted.

Chapter 16, Section 4
GUIDED READING

A. Possible answers:

1. Permitted nations to buy U.S. armaments as long as they paid cash and carried the goods away in their own ships

2. Japan, Germany, Italy; if the U.S. declared war on any of the Axis powers, it would have to fight a two-ocean war.

3. Allowed the president to lend or lease arms and supplies to "any country whose defense was vital to the U.S."

4. Punished Japan with a trade embargo

5. Collective security, disarmament, self-determination, economic cooperation, freedom of the Jews

6. An alliance of 26 nations that had joined together to fight the Axis powers

7. Almost destroyed it

8. They had signed a mutual defense treaty with Japan in which they agreed to come to each other's aid in the event of an attack.

Chapter 16
BUILDING VOCABULARY

A.

1. f	5. a
2. h	6. b
3. g	7. c
4. e	8. d

B.

1. totalitarian

2. fascism

3. *blitzkrieg*

4. Axis Powers

5. Lend-Lease Act

C. Answers will vary depending on the specifics noted.

Chapter 16, Section 2
SKILLBUILDER PRACTICE

Possible responses:

1. Appeals: the unfairness of England having more space for fewer people than Germany had; making sacrifices for national unity; making Germany rich and beautiful; having the best culture

2. Needs and views: a need to feel their people and country were strong, especially after being pulled apart following World War I; a

strong nationalistic view; entering into war only if it was necessary to protect the State.

Chapter 16, Section 1
RETEACHING ACTIVITY

1. d

2. b

3. a

4. a

5. d

6. d

Chapter 16, Section 2
RETEACHING ACTIVITY

A.

1. 3

2. 6

3. 1

4. 4

5. 2

6. 5

B.

1. nonaggression pact

2. Poland

3. phony war

4. natural resources

5. air force

Chapter 16, Section 3
RETEACHING ACTIVITY

1. The Nazis blamed the Jews for many of Germany's failures, including its economic problems and defeat in World War I.

2. A two-day assault by the Nazis ensued on Jewish homes, businesses, and synagogues in which about 100 Jews were killed and many more injured.

3. Many Americans feared that letting in more refugees in the midst of the Great Depression would deny Americans jobs and threaten economic recovery.

4. Some formed resistance move-

ments, while others published underground newspapers, set up secret schools to continue educating Jewish children, and kept alive various cultural activities, such as theater and music.

5. The effort to kill the entire population of Jews to keep them from destroying the purity of the "master race" of Aryans

6. Gassing, shooting, hanging, poisoning, and medical experiments

Chapter 16, Section 4
RETEACHING ACTIVITY

A.

Lend-Lease—allowed the nation to lend or lease arms and other supplies to "any country whose defense was vital to the United States"; Atlantic Charter—established a U.S.-British declaration of war aims: collective security, disarmament, self-determination, economic cooperation, and freedom of the seas; Pearl Harbor attack—shocked and angered Americans and prompted the United States to enter the war

B.

1. Congress boosted defense spending and passed the nation's first peacetime military draft, while Roosevelt sought to provide more aid to the Allies.

2. It cut off trade with Japan and withheld its precious oil supplies to the nation.

3. The Japanese viewed the U.S. navy as the main obstacle in their plans to create an empire in the Pacific region.

Chapter 16, Section 4
GEOGRAPHY APPLICATION

Responses may vary on the inferential questions. Sample responses are given for those.

1. Japan controlled Korea, the southern half of Sakhalin Island, the Kuril Islands, and the island of Taiwan.

2. The region of Manchuria in China; since it controlled Korea, Japan already had territory on Manchuria's

border, making the move into Manchuria an easy one.

3. Japan controlled much of eastern China, including the major cities of Beijing and Shanghai.

4. The Japanese could attack nearby Southeast Asian countries—Thailand, Malaya, and the Dutch East Indies—without needing to transport troops and equipment all the way from Japan itself.

5. Taiwan

6. Pearl Harbor

7. The Philippines would form a sort of barrier, shielding Japanese-held territory in Southeast Asia from U.S. attack and permitting Japanese expansion in that region to proceed unchecked.

Chapter 16, Section 1
PRIMARY SOURCE

Franklin D. Roosevelt's "Quarantine Speech"

1. He believed that the United States could not be insulated from "economic and political upheavals in the rest of the world" because the modern world was technically and morally interdependent.

2. Students will likely cite specific acts of aggression committed by Fascists in Italy, by Nazis in Germany, and by militarists in Japan.

3. Students' opinions will vary but should be supported by reasons that address Roosevelt's points.

Chapter 16, Section 4
PRIMARY SOURCE

The Bombing of Pearl Harbor

1. Through their research, students may find that American officials had broken Japanese diplomatic and military codes and were aware of Japan's plan to begin military operations against the United States in December. However, the naval base at Pearl Harbor received Washington's message to prepare for war too late and Japan's formal declaration of war arrived 50 minutes late. Also, they may learn that base commanders believed that

Hawaii was too far from Japan to be a target for an attack, and military advisers expected an attack at British Malaya, Thailand, or the Philippines. Students may find that Roosevelt asked Congress for a declaration of war against Japan the day after the attack and received unanimous approval in the Senate in 15 minutes and approval in the House after 40 minutes with just one dissenting vote, that of Montana's Jeannette Rankin.

2. Students will likely say that Roosevelt's remarks following the attack on Pearl Harbor reflect a similar position to the one he expressed in his "quarantine speech": it is impossible for the United States to isolate itself and avoid the consequences of "world lawlessness." Some students may point out that the president's remarks following the attack on Pearl Harbor, however, were far more forceful and direct since he was calling for war against Japan.

3. Before students begin, suggest that the class work together to compose a letter to the Hawaii Visitors Bureau in Honolulu requesting information about the memorial on Oahu. Informally assess how students' original ideas compare with the actual Pearl Harbor memorial.

Chapter 16, Section 4
PRIMARY SOURCE

War Poster

1. Students may point out the persuasive slogans "Avenge Pearl Harbor" and "Our bullets will do it" and the images of a defiant Uncle Sam shaking his fist at Japanese bombers over Pearl Harbor.

2. Responses will vary but may include any of the following: patriotism, anger, fear, a desire for revenge, aggression, outrage, panic.

3. Students might say that this poster illustrates the nation's commitment to war with Japan and fighting against unprovoked attacks on U.S. soil.

Chapter 16, Section 3
LITERATURE SELECTION

Sophie's Choice

1. Taken prisoner during a roundup of Polish members of the underground Resistance movement, she was mistakenly suspected of being a subversive.

2. Sophie had to choose which child—her son Jan or her daughter Eva—would be sent to the gas chamber and which she could keep.

3. Some students will agree that Sophie had to make a choice rather than risk losing both of her children. They may suggest that Sophie chose to keep her son because she felt he was older and had a better chance of surviving life in a concentration camp. Other students will agree that Sophie had to make a choice under the circumstances but may question her decision to keep her son and send her daughter to her death. A few students may not agree with Sophie's actions. They may feel that she should have refused the doctor's orders, even if it meant losing her own life or the lives of both her children, because she will always be haunted by the choice she has made.

Chapter 16, Section 3
AMERICAN LIVES

Elie Wiesel

Possible responses:

1. Wiesel means that those who forget the evil of the Holocaust are ignoring the suffering of the people who died, which is the same as helping to kill them.

2. Wiesel is like a conscience, reminding people of the evil of persecuting others, and like a warning signal, cautioning others to be on guard against intolerance.

3. Words can move people to do good or evil, and they can live on in books and memories, which makes them as powerful as actions.

Chapter 16, Section 4
AMERICAN LIVES

Charles A. Lindbergh

Possible responses:

1. He lost his privacy.

2. Lindbergh believed that the United States had no connection with Europe because its borders ended with the oceans.

3. He withdrew from the America First Committee because his remarks, which seemed to be anti-Semitic, made him seem racist and no longer credible or desirable as a speaker.

Chapter 17, Section 1
GUIDED READING

A. Possible answers:

1. Selective Service: Instituted the draft, providing the country with about 10 million soldiers

2. Women: Thousands served in the WAAC and other auxiliary branches; 6 million went to work in war industries.

3. Minorities: More than 300,000 Mexican Americans, more than a million African Americans, and tens of thousands of Asian Americans and Native Americans enlisted in the armed forces.

4. Manufacturers: Converted factories to production of war goods; built and expanded shipyards and defense plants

5. Randolph: Organized a march on Washington that forced President Roosevelt to issue an executive order calling on employers and labor unions in defense industries to stop discriminating against workers

6. OSRD: Spurred improvements in radar and sonar; encouraged the use of pesticides to fight insects; pushed the development of "miracle drugs" that saved lives; developed the atomic bomb

7. Entertainment: Churned out war-oriented propaganda films; created opportunities to escape from the grim realities of war for a few hours

8. OPA: Fought inflation by freezing prices on most goods; set up a system for rationing scarce goods

9. WPB: Oversaw the conversion from peacetime to wartime production; allocated raw materials to key industries; organized nationwide scrap drives

10. Rationing: Reduced consumption of energy, goods, and supplies deemed essential for the military

B. George Marshall pushed for the formation of a Women's Auxiliary Army Corps, so that women could perform certain duties then being done by soldiers.

Nisei were Japanese Americans born in the U.S.; before Pearl Harbor, thousands of them were drafted; after Pearl Harbor, thousands were shipped to internment camps.

Chapter 17, Section 2
GUIDED READING

A. Possible answers:

1. Stalingrad: Prevented Germany from taking over the Soviet Union; marked the point from which the Soviet Army began to move westward toward Germany

2. Operation Torch: Placed the Allies in control of North Africa; gave the Allies a place to launch an attack against Italy

3. Atlantic: Safeguarded Allied shipping of war materials to Europe

4. D-Day: Allied invasion of Europe; the liberation of Europe begins

5. Majdanek: First death camp liberated by Allied forces

6. France: Freed the country from four years of Nazi occupation

7. Aachen: First German town captured by the Americans

8. Bulge: From this point on, Germany could do little but retreat.

9. Italian: Resulted in freedom for Italy and the execution of Mussolini

10. V-E Day: The unconditional surrender of Germany; the end of war

in Europe

B. Answers will vary widely depending upon the specifics noted.

Chapter 17, Section 3
GUIDED READING

A. Possible answers:

1. Bataan: (Douglas) MacArthur; the Allies held out for four months against invading Japanese forces before abandoning the peninsula.

2. Midway: (Chester W.) Nimitz; Americans turned back a Japanese invasion force headed for Hawaii.

3. Guadalcanal: MacArthur; Americans dealt Japan its first defeat on land.

4. Leyte Gulf: MacArthur; Americans retook the Philippines and dealt a devastating blow to the Japanese navy.

5. Iwo Jima: MacArthur; in a fierce battle, the Allies took the island from Japan.

6. Okinawa: MacArthur; the Allies took the island from Japan.

7. Tokyo Bay: Hirohito, MacArthur; Japan formally surrendered.

8. Los Alamos: (J. Robert) Oppenheimer; the first atomic bomb was built, successfully completing Manhattan Project.

9. Hiroshima and Nagasaki: Truman; first atomic bombs were dropped.

10. Yalta: Roosevelt, Stalin, Churchill; at the Yalta Conference, Allied leaders made important decisions about the postwar world.

11. San Francisco: United Nations (UN) established

12. Nuremberg: Jackson; at the Nuremberg trials, Nazi leaders were tried for wartime crimes.

B. Answers will vary widely depending upon the specifics noted.

Chapter 17, Section 4
GUIDED READING

A. Possible answers:

1. Labor: Unemployment fell; average

weekly paychecks rose; women entered the workforce in record numbers and were then forced out of it after the war; women and minorities were offered better pay and more challenging jobs.

2. Agriculture: Farm machinery and fertilizers improved; crop prices, crop production, and farm income increased; many farmers were able to pay off their mortgages.

3. Population centers: The population of states, cities, and towns with military bases and defense industries increased dramatically.

4. Family life: The number of women juggling work and family (and raising children alone) increased dramatically; the marriage rate increased dramatically.

5. Returning GIs: GI Bill of Rights dramatically increased the standard of living of many GIs by providing free education and job training, as well as federal loan guarantees for buying homes and farms or starting businesses.

6. African Americans: Defended their nation by joining the military and working in defense industries; founded the Congress of Racial Equality (CORE); staged sit-ins; founded committees to improve race relations

7. Mexican Americans: Defended their nation by joining the military; the zoot suit rebellion against tradition

8. Japanese Americans: Defended their nation by joining the military; fought against forced relocation; founded the Japanese Americans Citizens League (JACL); sought compensation for those forced into internment camps

B. Answers will vary widely depending upon the specifics noted.

Chapter 17
BUILDING VOCABULARY

A.

1. b

2. a

3. c

4. c

5. c

B.

F—George Marshall was instrumental in the formation of the Women's Auxiliary Army Corps; or James Farmer was instrumental in the formation of the Congress of Racial Equality.

F—The Battle of Midway was considered a turning point in the battle against the Japanese.

T

T

F—The Manhattan Project was the code name of the effort to develop an atomic bomb.

C. Answers will vary depending on the specifics noted.

Chapter 17, Section 1
SKILLBUILDER PRACTICE

Possible responses:

Positive words: sturdy, patriots, land of the free, steely courage, scientific miracles, living flame

Negative words: wishy-washy, wishful thinking

Idealized descriptions and images: loyal women folk, backbone that shows whenever the chips are down, our great democratic nation, fight to the last ditch in friendly fierceness, personal privilege to think and dream

Chapter 17, Section 1
RETEACHING ACTIVITY

A.

1. African Americans

2. women

3. inflation

4. atomic bomb

5. rationing

B.

1. They worked as nurses, ambulance drivers, radio operators, electricians, and pilots.

2. Many abandoned production of their normal goods and put out much-needed war supplies.

3. It created the Office of Price

Administration, which froze the prices on many goods to control inflation, and the War Production Board, which oversaw the nation's conversion to a wartime production.

Chapter 17, Section 2
RETEACHING ACTIVITY

A.

1. 6

2. 3

3. 5

4. 1

5. 4

6. 2

B.

1. F—Adolf Hitler committed suicide shortly before Germany's surrender.

2. T

3. T

4. F—The leader of Germany Afrika Korps was Erwin Rommel, the legendary Desert Fox.

5. T

Chapter 17, Section 3
RETEACHING ACTIVITY

1. b

2. c

3. a

4. a

5. d

6. d

Chapter 17, Section 4
RETEACHING ACTIVITY

1. More than one million people moved to California for war-related jobs, and record numbers of African Americans left the South for war-related jobs in the North.

2. It provided college education and training for veterans and provided them with loans to buy homes or start new businesses.

3. To battle the policy of urban segre-

gation in the North

4. Several nights of anti-Mexican violence in Los Angeles that started after U.S. sailors claimed they were attacked by Mexicans in zoot-suit style of dress

5. Many of them were viewed as a security threat and thus rounded up and placed in internment camps

6. The internment of Japanese-Americans was justified on the basis of "military necessity."

Chapter 17, Section 2
GEOGRAPHY APPLICATION

Responses may vary on the inferential questions. Sample responses are given for those.

1. to show the effects of the Allied bombing of Dresden

2. the inner city

3. the autobahn, the main railroad yard, the railroad lines, the bridges across the Elbe River, the factories and gasworks, the infantry barracks, and the military transport headquarters

4. only the military transport headquarters

5. in areas outside the inner city

6. It may have have been intended to terrorize the residents of Dresden rather than to destroy military targets, so that Germany would surrender out of fear that similar destruction would be inflicted on civilians in other German cities.

7. It can be said with certainty only that Dresden was no longer an "intact government center." The infantry barracks, the autobahn, and the bridges were left virtually untouched.

8. Since the bombing appears to have had no strategic purpose, the destruction of central Dresden merely for the sake of punishment and revenge seems excessive and beneath the dignity of the Allied forces.

Chapter 17, Section 2
OUTLINE MAP

1. Great Britain and the Soviet Union

2. Switzerland, Spain, Portugal, Sweden, Turkey, and Saudi Arabia

3. Possible response: The Axis was seemingly in very good shape. Its control reached areas deep into the eastern part of Europe, and it faced only a hostile Great Britain to the north and west, with no threat from the south.

4. Possible response: Axis control of Great Britain would most likely have prevented the United States from entering the war, since there would have been no base for U.S. operations in Europe. This could have ensured an Axis victory in World War II.

5. Possible response: It gave the Allies a way to strike at the Axis from the south, thereby diverting Axis men and supplies and preventing a deeper push into the Soviet Union or a possible invasion of Great Britain.

Chapter 17, Section 1
PRIMARY SOURCE

War Ration Stamps

1. To identify the person so as to reduce the possibility of fraud or black market trading

2. $10,000 fine, imprisonment, or both

3. Students may point out that most Americans accepted rationing because they had no choice if they wanted to buy scarce items. They may also say that many Americans were motivated by patriotism and wanted to help the United States military during the war. A few students may mention that the penalties for violating rationing regulations might have compelled some Americans to accept the rationing system.

Chapter 17, Section 2
PRIMARY SOURCE

War Dispatch from Ernie Pyle

1. Informally assess students' letters on the basis of creativity, coherency,

and historical accuracy.

2. Before students begin this activity, have them draw up a list of questions they would like to ask and set up a time for the interview. If students do not know someone who served in World War II, guide them to contact a local branch of the Veterans of Foreign Wars. As an alternative to this activity, you may want to invite a World War II veteran to speak to the class about his experiences.

3. Informally assess students' photo essays. Invite them to display their work in the classroom.

Chapter 17, Section 3
PRIMARY SOURCE

The Bombing of Nagasaki

1. Through their research, students may find that the uranium bomb dropped on Hiroshima, code named "Little Boy," killed approximately 70,000 people, injured about 68,000, and flattened about four square miles of the city. The plutonium bomb named "Fat Man" that was dropped on Nagasaki killed about 40,000 people, injured about 40,000, and obliterated nearly half of the city. The effects of radiation from the two bombs later killed another 100,000 people, approximately.

2. Informally assess students' debates. You may want to encourage them to role-play particular individuals who took an active part in this debate, such as General Dwight D. Eisenhower who opposed the bombings; Leo Szilard who felt the Japanese should have fair warning before the atomic bomb was used; and President Truman and Secretary of War Henry Stimson who supported the bombings.

Chapter 17, Section 4
PRIMARY SOURCE

Farewell to Manzanar

1. The accommodations were 16-by-20-foot shacks of pine boards covered with tarpaper; each shack had one bare light bulb and an oil stove for heat. Furnishings consisted of

army cots, blankets, and mattress covers.

2. Some students may say that the shacks were hastily put up because there wasn't enough time to construct anything well. However, most students will probably realize that the main reason for the poor accommodations was the strong anti-Japanese feeling at the time. Japanese-Americans were being punished for the attack on Pearl Harbor.

3. Caucasian servers poured fruit over the rice served to prisoners, thinking it would make a good dessert; however, among the Japanese rice is eaten only with salty or savory foods, never with sweet. Just as incorrect assumptions were made about Japanese dietary customs, so on a greater scale, were false assumptions made regarding regarding whether or not Japanese Americans actually posed a threat to national security during World War II; the lack of understanding resulted in their internment.

Chapter 17, Section 4
LITERATURE SELECTION

Snow Falling on Cedars

1. Before students begin, encourage them to focus on either the economic, social, or psychological impact of internment. Then informally assess students' oral reports on the basis of accuracy as well as the quality of their research and writing.

2. Students' maps may include the following: Topaz, Utah; Posten and Gila River, Arizona; Heart Mountain, Wyoming; Tule Lake and Manzanar, California; Minidoka, Idaho; Granada, Colorado; Rohwer and Jerome, Arkansas. After they are finished, you may want to hold a class discussion about why internment camps were situated in these locations.

Chapter 17, Section 1
AMERICAN LIVES

Oveta Culp Hobby

Possible responses:

1. Some people objected to the organization, and early reports on the

WACs dealt with trivial issues such as uniforms. Hobby had to point out that the purpose of the organization was important to the war effort.

2. Many people opposed creation of the WACs, and the women were limited to noncombat duty. While 100,000 women served in the unit in 1945, millions of men served. In today's army, women are much more widely accepted, and they are even allowed to serve in combat in certain situations.

3. Hobby is described as being in charge of a big-city newspaper, overseeing the WAC and being promoted to colonel, and guiding a large government agency through the major tests of desegregation and polio-vaccination distribution.

Chapter 17, Section 2
AMERICAN LIVES

George S. Patton

Possible responses:

1. Patton's skill as a commander is shown in how he rallied II Armored Corps to become an effective fighting force, by his rapid moves in Sicily, by the quick advance through northern France, and by the counterattack against the Germans after their last offensive.

2. Eisenhower put up with Patton's behavior and kept him in command because he appreciated his abilities to lead armies in combat.

3. When Patton urged an attack on the Soviet Union, that nation was still an ally. Also, he suggested joining with the German army for the attack, but Germany was still considered the allies' enemy.

Chapter 18, Section 1
GUIDED READING

A. Possible answers:

1. The Truman administration established a policy of containment to block further Soviet expansion.

2. The Truman Doctrine declared that the U.S. would support any free country that was resisting a takeover by an outside or an armed force.

3. The U.S. flew food and supplies into West Berlin during the Berlin airlift.

4. The U.S. joined ten other Western European nations in creating NATO, a defensive military alliance.

B. Answers will vary widely depending upon the specifics noted.

Chapter 18, Section 2
GUIDED READING

A. Possible answers:

1. China: Nationalists; because they opposed communism

   Korea: South Korea; because it was democratic and North Korea was Communist

2. China: sent the Nationalists billions of dollars in military equipment and supplies; tried to negotiate an end to the war

   Korea: provided naval and air support; sent troops; went to war

3. China: the Communists won the war, forcing the Nationalists to flee to Taiwan.

   Korea: stalemate; Korea remained two nations divided by a demilitarized zone; the United States lost 54,000 American lives and spent $67 billion.

4. China: with shock, anger, and fear; Americans couldn't believe that the policy of containment had failed and demanded explanations from the government.

   Korea: with dismay; the high costs of the unsuccessful war led Americans to reject the Democratic party.

B. Answers will vary widely depending upon the specifics noted.

Chapter 18, Section 3
GUIDED READING

A. Possible answers:

1. a. Accused of disloyalty; being Communists; exposing moviegoers to Communist propaganda

   b. They were imprisoned and blacklisted; their careers and reputations were destroyed.

   c. Students will hold various opinions regarding the fairness of the accusations.

2. a. Accused of spying for the Soviet Union; passing government documents to the Soviet Union; perjury

   b. He was convicted of perjury and jailed.

   c. Students will hold various opinions regarding the fairness of the accusations.

3. a. Accused of spying for the Soviet Union; helping to pass information to the Soviets about the atomic bomb

   b. They were convicted and executed.

   c. Students will hold various opinions regarding the fairness of the accusations.

4. McCarthy's desire to be reelected; the Republicans' desire to win the presidential election; growing fears of communism and suspicion of foreign influences in the United States.

5. McCarthy fed on the public's fears and gave the impression that he was purging the nation of a very dangerous, and seemingly very real, Communist menace.

6. In televised hearings, McCarthy bullied witnesses, turning the public against him. There was no proof for his accusations.

B. Answers will vary widely depending upon the specifics noted.

Chapter 18, Section 4
GUIDED READING

A. Possible answers:

1. With fear and horror because the Soviet Union's development of the atomic bomb took away the U.S. advantage in weaponry; decided to develop the H-bomb before the

Soviets did in order to regain military superiority

2. Used covert CIA action to topple the Iranian government in order to establish a government more favorable to Western interests

3. Used covert CIA action to topple the Guatemalan government in order to establish a government more favorable to Western interests

4. With shock because the situation didn't seem to call for aggression; to end the crisis, asked the UN to order a cease-fire and the withdrawal of troops.

5. Protested the invasion but could do little to help

6. With shock because it made Americans feel vulnerable to nuclear attack and inferior to Soviet science and technology; to regain superiority, the U.S. worked to improve education and to develop satellites and better weapons-delivery systems

7. At first, lied about the purpose of the flight to keep spying activities secret but then publicly admitted guilt to salvage an impending summit conference on the arms race.

B. Answers will vary widely depending upon the specifics noted.

Chapter 18
BUILDING VOCABULARY

A.

1. f	5. g
2. d	6. b
3. c	7. e
4. h	8. a

B.

1. a

2. c

3. b

4. c

5. a

C. Answers will vary depending on the specifics noted.

Chapter 18, Section 1
SKILLBUILDER PRACTICE

Responses will vary but should include points similar to the following:

The Soviet Union

• suffered more casualties and destruction than other Allies during the war.

• feared another invasion from the West.

• needed to rebuild itself and needed the military protection that the satellite nations provided.

The United States

• had considerably fewer casualties and less destruction than the Soviet Union.

• emerged from the war economically stronger than ever; feared totalitarian governments.

• needed free markets in Europe to sell the large amount of goods and services that it produced.

Chapter 18, Section 1
RETEACHING ACTIVITY

1. b

2. c

3. a

4. c

5. a

6. a

Chapter 18, Section 2
RETEACHING ACTIVITY

A.

June 1950—North Korean forces sweep across the 38th parallel, starting the Korean War; September 1950—U.S. troops arrive and push the North Koreans back above the 38th parallel; January 1951—North Korean forces repel the Allied forces and a bloody stalemate ensues; June 1951—the two sides agree to a cease-fire

B.

1. Republicans and Democrats alike criticized the Truman administration for not providing enough support to China; many Americans began to fear a world-wide spread of communism.

2. MacArthur continued to criticize Truman publicly over his handling of the war in Korea.

3. The failure in Korea led Americans to reject the Democratic Party and elect a Republican to the White House in 1952.

Chapter 18, Section 3
RETEACHING ACTIVITY

A.

Hollywood Ten—A group of Hollywood workers refused to help investigators on an anti-Communist crusade in the movie industry and were sent to prison; many other Hollywood workers were blacklisted due to alleged Communist ties; Rosenberg Trial—Ethel and Julius Rosenberg, minor activists in the American Communist Party, were convicted of espionage on what many believed was weak evidence and sentenced to death; McCarthyism—U.S. Senator Joseph McCarthy engaged in a reckless anti-Communist crusade, often publicly accusing people of Communist ties and ruining their reputations often without any evidence.

B.

1. T

2. F—Richard Nixon first rose to popularity by pursuing charges against alleged State Department spy Alger Hiss.

3. F—Joseph McCarthy's downfall came after he made Communist-related accusations against the U.S. Army.

Chapter 18, Section 4
RETEACHING ACTIVITY

A.

1. c

2. f

3. e

4. b

5. d

6. a

B.

1. Hungary

2. Eisenhower Doctrine

3. space race

4. Israel

5. brinkmanship

Chapter 18, Section 1
GEOGRAPHY APPLICATION

Responses may vary on the inferential questions. Sample responses are given for those.

1. food

2. Britain and France; because they were our most important allies during the war. They also suffered great damage, had large populations, and therefore needed more aid for recovery.

3. Possible response: The Soviets felt that the United States would use the Marshall Plan to break their hold over their satellite countries in Eastern Europe.

4. slightly more than $200 million

5. Britain; just over $1 billion

6. Soviet aggression in Czechoslovakia; the United States feared that Communists might gain control of more European countries.

7. Possible response: The lure of communism has proved especially strong when people are starving. The Marshall Plan helped end hunger in Western Europe and, therefore, helped save that area from falling under Soviet domination.

Chapter 18, Section 1
PRIMARY SOURCE

Truman's Letter to His Daughter

1. Truman faced the challenge of being very ignorant about the war and foreign affairs in general when he became president because Roosevelt had told him very little. He also didn't know how to handle the Soviets and may have mistakenly trusted them to abide by earlier agreements. Finally, Truman was challenged with establishing the peace of the world with a very

uncooperative Soviet partner.

2. Truman seems to have really distrusted and disliked the Soviet government because he considered it totalitarian.

3. Many students may think that Truman did the best that he could, given his initial ignorance. Some may point out that he should have been harder on the Soviets.

Chapter 18, Section 2
PRIMARY SOURCE

MacArthur's Farewell Address

1. Some students may feel that MacArthur's argument for expanding the war into China without using U.S. ground forces is the most persuasive. Others may feel his argument for decisive military action is most convincing. For some students, MacArthur's remarks at the beginning of his speech arguing that he is not an "advocate for any partisan cause" is the least persuasive.

2. Some students may think that MacArthur sounds angry and bitter in his speech; others may say he is forceful and passionate about his beliefs. Support for students' opinions should be examples of the strong language he uses in the address.

3. Responses will vary but should be thoughtful and supported.

Chapter 18, Section 4
PRIMARY SOURCE

Eisenhower's Statement on the U-2 Incident

1. Eisenhower says that spying on the Soviets is justified because the U.S. needs to be aware of what the Soviet military is doing so that we can prepare to defend and/or protect the country.

2. Some students will agree and support their opinions with reasons similar to Eisenhower's. Others may disagree and cite the increased hostilities between the two countries and their subsequent military buildups to prove their point.

Chapter 18, Section 4,
LITERATURE SELECTION

The Nuclear Age

1. During their research, students may find that the potential effects of nuclear war in the 1950s were not as dangerous as they would become later. It might have been possible for some families to survive an A-bomb attack depending upon how far they were away from the blast site. Students may also find that many of the ingredients in William's mask and shelter are correct, namely the charcoal and the lead shield. However, they will also discover that a ping-pong table is no match for an A-bomb.

2. Students who choose this activity may discover that some of the ingredients in William's mask and shelter were similar to what some people were actually using to protect themselves at that time.

Chapter 18, Section 2
AMERICAN LIVES

Douglas MacArthur

Possible responses:

1. MacArthur wanted to project an image of a stylish, even dashing, soldier and a bold leader, which he conveyed with his flashy dress and inspirational messages.

2. Because he lived outside the U.S. for so many years, MacArthur wasn't used to civilian politics and authority. This may have lead him to challenge Truman.

3. Americans may have favored Eisenhower over MacArthur because they were disturbed by MacArthur's challenge to presidential authority, something Eisenhower never did.

Chapter 18, Section 3
AMERICAN LIVES

Margaret Chase Smith

Possible responses:

1. She supported the Lend-Lease Act and the Selective Service Act in the 1940s and voted for federal aid to

education, health insurance for older people, and some civil rights laws in the 1950s.

2. McCarthy, protecting himself with the freedom of speech, had scared others into not speaking out against him.

3. Smith was more politically moderate and more personally honorable that McCarthy. While she criticized Democratic policies, she did not charge Democrats with disloyalty. McCarthy used degrading and disrespectful language, such as calling her and her supporters "Snow White and the Seven Dwarfs."

Chapter 19, Section 1
GUIDED READING

A. Possible answers:

1. Truman and Congress: GI Bill of Rights (free education, unemployment benefits, low-interest loans)

2. Developers: Mass-produced, standardized homes built using assembly-line methods

   Congress: Financial support to clear out slums and build low-income housing units; increased funding for public housing

3. Truman and Congress: Reestablishment of wartime controls on prices, wages, and rents

4. Truman: Threatens to draft strikers

5. Truman: Federal anti-lynching law; abolition of the poll tax as a voting requirement; establishment of a permanent body to prevent racial discrimination in hiring; passage of federal legislation to eliminate discrimination in voting; integration of the armed forces

B. Answers will vary widely depending upon the specifics noted.

Chapter 19, Section 2
GUIDED READING

A. Possible answers:

1. Business: Standardized what people ate; offered economic advancement to people who would conform; offered job security to more Americans; contributed to the baby

boom and suburbanization; offered consumers more choices

2. Suburban: Offered people the chance to live the American dream; caused many Americans, especially women, to feel dissatisfied with their lives; contributed to the popularity of the automobile; led to the decline of cities; created racial and economic gulfs between suburban and city dwellers

3. Population: Created the largest generation in U.S. history; contributed to suburbanization and business expansion; led to widespread overcrowding in schools and a teacher shortage; led to a boom in activities geared toward youth

4. Leisure: Contributed to business expansion in leisure fields; gave people time to engage in a wide variety of recreational pursuits; helped to increase sales of books and magazines

5. Automobile: Spurred the building of roads and interstate highways; encouraged suburbanization and urban decline; helped the trucking industry to take business from the railroads; helped to unify and homogenize the nation; offered Americans more possibilities for leisure activities; stimulated other industries; created noise and air pollution; led to more traffic jams and accidents

6. Consumerism: Helped to popularize the equating of material goods with success; contributed to the expansion of business; encouraged manufacturers to produce a wider variety of goods; encouraged planned obsolescence and the "throwaway society"; caused an increase in private debt; led to a boom in the advertising industry

B. Answers will vary widely depending upon the specifics noted.

Chapter 19, Section 3
GUIDED READING

A. Possible answers:

1. a. TV Shows: *I Love Lucy; See It Now; Playhouse 90*

   b. Subjects presented: Comedy; idealized white America; Western frontier

c. Subjects avoided: Poverty; diversity; contemporary conflicts, such as racial discrimination

2. a. Radio changes: Turned to local programming; began targeting specialized audiences

   b. African-American culture: Hundreds of stations focused on African-American performers, helping to sell their records.

3. Film: Introduced innovations such as stereoscopic sound and Cinema-Scope to capitalize on its advantages over TV; introduced such fads as piped-in smells and 3-D

4. a. Beat movement: Ginsberg, Kerouac

   b. Characteristics: Nonconformity; antimaterialism; interest in a higher consciousness; the shunning of structure in life and art

5. a. Rock 'n' roll: Freed, Presley, Berry, Little Richard; radio, TV

   b. Characteristics: heavy rhythm; simple melodies and lyrics; focus on youth

B. Answers will vary widely depending upon the specifics noted.

Chapter 19, Section 4
GUIDED READING

A. Possible answers:

Decaying cities

1. Causes: "White flight"; suburbanization; remaining city residents poorer than those that left; loss of property and income taxes; a decrease in the quality of services

2. Effects: Rundown neighborhoods torn down; cleared areas not always used for housing, which led to housing shortages

Mexican Americans

3. Solutions: The creation of the American G.I. Forum, the Unity League of California, and voter registration groups in other states

Native Americans

4. Causes: A termination policy adopted by the federal government

5. Solutions: The Bureau of Indian

Affairs began a voluntary relocation program to help Native Americans find a place to live and work and to pay for moving and living expenses.

6. Effects: Only 35,000 Native Americans relocated in the program; many of them were unable to find jobs; the number of Native Americans on state welfare rolls soared

B. Answers will vary widely depending upon the specifics noted.

Chapter 19
BUILDING VOCABULARY

A.

1. e   5. d
2. f   6. c
3. g   7. b
4. h   8. a

B.

1. F—Under the termination policy, the federal government took less responsibility for Native American tribes.

2. T

3. T

4. F—The Federal Communications Commission was charged with regulating and licensing the various communications industries.

5. T

C. Answers will vary depending on the specifics noted.

Chapter 19, Section 3
SKILLBUILDER PRACTICE

Possible responses:

1. *Time* magazine

2. The source is a respected news magazine. We don't know anything about the author actually, so can't say what his/her qualifications are.

3. Tone is sarcastic, disapproving, belittling, humorous.

4. Although there are quite a few facts in the article, opinions predominate. The first paragraph is a series of facts and the information on the ori-

gin of rock 'n' roll is factual. Opinions include: "It does for music what a motorcycle club . . . Sunday afternoon;" "the blues with malice aforethought;" "sounds like a bull whip;" "a choleric saxophone honking mating-call sounds;" "a near-nonsense phrase;" "a moronic lyric;" "it makes a virtue out of monotony;" "It's just not couth."

5. Yes, it reflects what most adults were thinking and shows the impact of rock 'n' roll on American culture.

No, it is too one-sided and full of one person's opinion to be typical of the times.

Chapter 19, Section 1
RETEACHING ACTIVITY

1. Americans went on a tremendous spending spree after going without many goods for years because of the war. Meanwhile, increased defense spending kept many people employed and a rebuilt Europe helped create strong foreign markets for U.S. goods.

2. He issued an executive order that integrated the armed forces and ordered an end to discrimination in the hiring of government employees.

3. Republicans gained control of both houses of Congress and passed the Taft-Hartley Act, which overturned many rights won by unions during the New Deal.

4. It refused to pass many of the president's measures, including public housing, federal aid to education, a higher minimum wage, and greater Social Security coverage.

5. Congress defeated the Fair Deal measures of mandatory health insurance and aid for farmers, but passed its other measures calling for an increase in the hourly wage, greater Social Security benefits, environmental projects, and urban renewal.

6. A middle road in which he vowed to be conservative on fiscal matter and liberal on social matters

Chapter 19, Section 2
RETEACHING ACTIVITY

1. Americans moves away from blue-collar to white-collar jobs as America witnesses the rise of conglomerates, franchises and other companies. This in turn leads to the rise of company men, or employees who put their interest in economic advancement and following society's rules over their own individuality.

2. A baby boom creates a need for more housing and soon suburban communities spring up around the nation's cities. Husbands travel to the city for work, while most women take on the role of homemaker. Meanwhile, Americans engage in more leisure activities, including sports and reading.

3. Suburban living makes owning a car a necessity as there is little in the way of public transportation. As a result, car ownership skyrockets. To accommodate so many new cars, the Eisenhower administration passes the Interstate Highways Act, which creates some 41,000 miles of national highways. The booming auto industry leads to the growth of numerous related industries as well as a rise in traffic jams and pollution.

4. Dozens of new products appear in the marketplace, as Americans buy numerous new items, from lawnmowers to barbecue grills, to compliment their suburban lifestyle. Manufactures promote even more buying through a strategy of planned obsolescence, in which they purposefully design products to become obsolete in a short period of time. Furthermore, this period of intense buying is accompanied by the growth of the advertising industry, with advertisers spending some $9 billion in 1955.

Chapter 19, Section 3
RETEACHING ACTIVITY

A.

1. c

2. d

3. f

4. e

5. b

6. a

B.

1. racism, poverty

2. African Americans

3. television

4. conformity

5. western

Chapter 19, Section 4
RETEACHING ACTIVITY

1. a

2. c

3. c

4. b

5. a

6. d

Chapter 19, Section 2
GEOGRAPHY APPLICATION

Responses may vary on the inferential questions. Sample responses are given for those.

1. The number of births declined for those years.

2. World War II had just ended, and U.S. servicemen who returned to civilian life were anxious to start families or to add to the families they already had.

3. 4.30—millions of births in the U.S. for that year; 4.60—millions of new Americans, from births and immigration; 1.66—millions of U.S. deaths for the year; by 2.94 million

4. A steep decline in births between 1964 and 1965 of more than 200,000 offset the increase in immigration.

5. In 1972 the number of births fell below that of the first year of the baby boom for the first time; perhaps because in 1965 the number of births fell below 4 million for the first time since 1954 and the 4-million level was considered a benchmark, or because in 1965 the birthrate fell below 20 per 1,000 people for the first time since 1941

and the rate of 20 was considered a benchmark.

6. The annual numbers of births fluctuated widely during the period, whereas the annual numbers of deaths were fairly consistent, remaining relatively steady until 1955 and then rising slowly over the next 20 years.

Chapter 19, Section 1
PRIMARY SOURCE

Cartoon

Possible responses:

1. stark, sterile, uniform, vast, overwhelming, cramped, impersonal, unappealing

2. Students may infer that because she does not know where she lives, she may feel frustrated, confused, upset, overwhelmed, or dissatisfied. As an extension activity, you may wish to have students write dialogue between Mrs. Barnes and a neighbor.

3. Students may suggest the following advantages: affordability, availability of housing during the housing shortage, accessibility to cities and services, sociability, security, and achievability of the American dream.

Chapter 19, Section 2
PRIMARY SOURCE

The Organization Man

Possible responses:

1. belonging to an organization, belonging to the middle class, living in suburbia, believing in the harmony between the individual and the organization

2. The American faith in hard work and individual effort is in conflict with the collective mentality needed in an organization. Whyte feels that individuality is diminished, if not lost, by being beholden to an organization, part of the "rat race," and unable to control one's own direction in life.

3. Most students will agree that there are organization people today, citing specific examples of people who work for corporations or belong to

other institutions. Some might point out that the growth of personal computers in the '80s and '90s has offered people more options, such as starting their own businesses or working out of their homes.

Chapter 19, Section 4
PRIMARY SOURCE

The Other America

1. In the year 2000, according to Bureau of the Census statistics, about 34 million individuals in the United States lived below the poverty level. These statistics indicate a slight decline in the number of poor Americans since the 1950s.

2. Informally assess students' charts. Through their research, they may list such programs as urban renewal, Job Corps, Project Head Start, Legal Services for the Poor, Upward Bound, Volunteers in Service to America, Model Cities, Medicaid, and Medicare.

Chapter 19, Section 4
PRIMARY SOURCE

The Voluntary Relocation Program

Possible responses:

1. the sterility and anonymity of a city restaurant; the friendly atmosphere of Wally's Bar where patrons call his brother "Indian Joe"; the sights, sounds, and smells of his brother's apartment building

2. He worked at Chicago Rawhide, lived in a fourth-floor apartment, and was a regular at Wally's Bar.

3. Students may infer that he felt unprepared for the challenges of city life, was overwhelmed by his unfamiliarity with Chicago, and missed the security of family life in Oklahoma.

4. Students will likely say the story reflects the program's failure; despite the government's attempt to help Native Americans resettle in cities, many returned to reservation life.

Chapter 19, Section 2
LITERATURE SELECTION

*The Man in the Gray
Flannel Suit*

1. The walls are damaged, the front door is scratched, the bathroom faucet drips, and the furniture is in poor condition. The house is small, ugly, and just like all the other houses on the block. Outside, the lawn is ragged, and the garden is full of weeds.

2. They discover that raising three children uses all the money they might have saved for a bigger house. They feel that the house is a trap, so they begin to hate it and do nothing to improve it.

3. Some students may say that their problem is their materialism, their view that comfort, pleasure, and wealth are life's most important goals. Others may say that their problem is fitting in and suppressing their individuality.

4. Students may point out that materialism is characteristic of several eras in U.S. history. Other postwar periods, such as the 1920s, witnessed economic growth and focused on materialistic goals. The 1980s was another time of plenty in the United States. They may also say that the pressure to conform has always existed in society in varying degrees.

Chapter 19, Section 3
LITERATURE SELECTION

1959

1. Informally assess students' rewritten passages.

2. Have students create Venn diagrams to compare music in the 1950s and the '00s. As an alternative, have them plan a Golden Oldies radio program featuring '50s music.

3. Informally assess students' dance demonstrations. You may want to have them demonstrate dance steps that are popular today to compare with these '50s dances.

Chapter 19, Section 1
AMERICAN LIVES

Jackie Robinson

Possible responses:

1. Rickey was looking for more than just talent. He needed to find someone with the character to withstand verbal abuse and adversity.

2. Robinson's breakthrough changed baseball—and most sports—by opening the doors to competition between nonwhite and white players.

3. Because baseball was an important part of popular culture at the time, his life helped show that racial discrimination was unfair.

Chapter 19, Section 3
AMERICAN LIVES

Milton Berle

Possible responses:

1. Berle did not succeed on radio because his visual humor could not be enjoyed by listeners.

2. Berle's popularity declined because changing television ownership patterns brought a larger audience that was less responsive to his humor. Also, constant exposure on television made his humor grow stale.

3. Celebrity can be fleeting and can disappear as public tastes change.

CURRICULUM